TRUST

FINDING FAITH WITHIN YOURSELF

BY TERRENCE SOUTHERN

FREILING
AGENCY

Cover Photo by Otis Clayborne of Clay Made Media

Published by Freiling Agency, LLC.

P.O. Box 1264
Warrenton, VA 20188

www.FreilingAgency.com

PB ISBN: 978-1-963701-31-9
E-book ISBN: 978-1-963701-32-6

DEDICATION

To my younger self, Thank you for the strength, resilience, and courage that brought me to this moment. You've carried the weight long enough—rest now, knowing I'll take it from here. And to my daughter, Zorah. You are my light, my inspiration, and my unwavering why.

CONTENTS

INTRODUCTION

"In complete darkness, we are all the same.
It is only our knowledge and wisdom that separates us.
Don't let your eyes deceive you"

—Janet Jackson

Every morning, I wake up to start my day by giving thanks to everything I have experienced that has brought me to where I am today. As I approach the door to enter the uncertain world that lacks trust, I only pray that I make it back home the same way or better than when I left. No matter what, my goal is to make it back home to my family. Can you relate?

For the last 25 years, I have poured my intellectual passion into the innovation of robotics technology in the industry and community and its impact on the future before us. I am often asked about my views on artificial intelligence, robotics, and automation. Can you trust them? Believe it or not, there are moments when I have more trust in the robotics solutions I have developed than I do people. Unlike robots, trust is not automated.

You see, robotics isn't something I found; it found me. While trust is something that had to grow on me over the years as I found my way through the darkness. Just a year before I began my journey to becoming a pioneering black robotics engineer, I attended a 5-day workshop presented by Landmark Education in Detroit, MI. I didn't want to be there, but my mother forced me to go. There were only a total of 5 kids there, including myself; the other 250 people were adults of all ages. What was the purpose? What did I gain from this forum? On the final day, all I could think was GET ME OUT OF HERE. Just before lunch, the entire group did a meditation exercise. I closed my eyes to participate, but I actually ended up falling asleep, only to be awakened by a middle-aged black man sitting next to me screaming at the top of his lungs while his eyes were still closed like he was being chased by Michael Myers. Then he began to chuckle as he opened his eyes briefly to look at me, and then he went back to meditating. I looked at him like bruh, what's your problem?

As we approached the end of the workshop, people were asked to share more about themselves and their experiences from the week. They decided to start with some of us young people because we had been so quiet most of the week. I was called on to share. I told them I was a college student studying engineering, and I spent a portion of my childhood mentoring a few of the boys in my neighborhood and loved playing basketball. To my surprise, the screaming black gentleman sitting next to me decided to share. He went to the front of the room to tell the group that during the meditation, he imagined that I had kidnapped and tortured him. He was not sure why he felt those thoughts since I seemed like a nice young man, and he was sorry. Next, an older white woman came up to share that when she saw me. She thought I was a violent man, and she was afraid. But after hearing me share my truths, she retracted her thoughts and apologized. Then, three more women came up to share similar thoughts about me, though none of them had ever spoken to me and only saw me throughout this week. It took me sharing my voice to change the trajectory of their mindset. Faith and fear both demand you believe in something you cannot see.

It's a weird world we live in. Did those individuals not trust me, or did they not trust themselves due to their own past experiences? Where were their internal truths and fears rooted? Where is it safe to tell the truth? What do people experience when they realize their thinking is all wrong? So many questions come to mind when attempting to understand how people get wired the way they are.

How did I get here? From being told I was the man of the house at the age of 5 to being held at gunpoint while a bookmobile was robbed at the age of 7 to being a contributor of negativity to the streets at the age of 14 to a notably accomplished Robotics Engineer. I reflect daily and give thanks to all who poured into me along the way. I'm simply blessed that a mentor strode into my life, brandishing the words "single-minded and focused" and "unusual sustained concentration."

Those words struck a chord deep within me.

Someone saw potential in me before I saw it in myself. This was the spark that ignited my path to trusting myself. But that was only the beginning of my story. It wasn't, and isn't, a smooth ride. There were craters and potholes aplenty. As more people uncover the intricacies of my story, their reaction is universal—that a person could endure so much and still find a reason to smile every day.

Trust is the silent architect of happiness. It is both fragile and steadfast—an invisible thread weaving through every relationship we hold dear, whether at work, in play, or at home. Maya Angelou once wrote, "Have enough courage to trust love one more time and always one more time." Her words resonate deeply, capturing the essence of what this book seeks to explore. Trust is not just a virtue; it's a necessity, a life force, and a mirror reflecting our hopes, fears, and resilience.

My aim with this book? To be your guide, just as others guided me. Great mentors are as rare as unicorns. Everyone needs a beacon—someone to toss the tough questions at, someone to dispense hard-but-necessary truths. That's the role I intend for this book to play in your life. My mentors saw a bigger picture in me than I saw in myself. In my eyes, I was just Terrence. I was initially skeptical of their insight. Trust wasn't my strong suit—not in them, not even in myself.

When there is a strong foundation of trust in an organization, it transforms the workplace through collaboration, teamwork, and honest communication. But trust extends far beyond professional settings. It is foundational in personal relationships and in the relationship we have with ourselves. This book will challenge you to ask: How easily do you grant your trust to others? What factors influence your ability—or inability—to trust specific individuals? And what do people need to do to earn your trust?

Trust is one of the most critical elements of healthy relationships, families, teams, organizations, and communities. Yet many of us have a disempowered relationship with it. We've been taught that trust must be earned when, in reality, trust is something we grant. How well do you trust yourself? For most of us, myself included, self-trust can be tricky. We second-guess ourselves. We don't listen to our gut or trust our instincts. We hang onto negative memories or regrets from the past, making it difficult to trust ourselves and, by extension, others.

But you're not alone. Lack of self-trust, while debilitating in many ways, is common. We all doubt ourselves sometimes—but that doesn't mean there's something wrong with us. It's perfectly normal. So, how do you stop doubting yourself and start living authentically with self-love, confidence, and truth? The first step is to notice and tell the truth about why it's difficult. Once we can honestly acknowledge our challenges (and have compassion for ourselves), we can consciously choose to trust ourselves in a more authentic way. Self-awareness and curiosity allow us to understand why we doubt ourselves, paving the way for growth.

Do you have trust issues? For some, a lack of trust stems from past betrayals, complicated relationships, or painful life experiences. These moments shape our ability to trust and often make it difficult to grant trust freely. As a Black man growing up in a world that often felt unkind and unforgiving, I learned early that trust wasn't something to be given lightly. My parents divorced when I was five, and mental and emotional struggles were a constant part of my family's story. Being a young Black boy in a tough neighborhood meant navigating spaces where trust often felt like a liability. My "street-smart survival kit" included a heavy dose of skepticism—a necessary shield for self-preservation.

This mindset served me well in some ways, helping me to stay safe and alert. But as I grew older, I realized that my reluctance to trust others was holding me back. Whether in relationships, friendships, or professional opportunities, I found myself building walls where bridges could have been. No matter how many "tests" I put people through, I eventually came to understand that trust wasn't about their actions; it was about my choice to let my guard down and believe in them.

Americans, by and large, don't trust each other. According to the General Social Survey, only one-third of Americans report trusting one another. This distrust extends beyond institutions to a fundamental lack of trust in people. What impact does this have on us? Political Scientist April K. Clark observes, "When trust is low, the way we react and behave with each other becomes less civil." While trust levels are often set by our mid-twenties, inspiring today's youth may offer hope for a more trusting society.

For African Americans, the legacy of systemic injustice adds complexity to trusting others. Racism, discrimination, and high poverty rates erode trust within communities. For many in the Black community, trust is not just a personal decision but a survival strategy shaped by lived experiences. My approach to trust was often shaped by past betrayals and societal barriers. But over time, I learned that withholding trust not only keeps others out but also keeps us locked in. When we refuse to trust, we limit our ability to connect, collaborate, and grow.

Will we get hurt by trusting? Yes. Will people let us down? Most certainly. But these experiences are inevitable, whether we freely grant trust or hold it back. The paradox is that the more we consciously grant trust, the more we create opportunities for genuine connection and collaboration.

Building trust takes courage. It requires a willingness to take risks, to forgive, and to see the best in others, even when it's hard. But when we do, we foster an environment where trust can thrive—in our relationships, families, workplaces, and communities. Isn't that what we're all ultimately seeking: to trust and to be trusted despite life's uncertainties?

This book is a journey—a chronicle of trust in all its forms. It delves into the gaps where trust falters and offers pathways to rebuild it stronger than before. At its heart are eighteen principles, born from my own life's tapestry. Some were stitched into me during my childhood in Detroit; others unfolded along my path to today. These principles are my offering to you—a tribute to the past, a beacon for the future.

As you turn these pages, I invite you to reflect on your own life and your untold stories of trust gained, lost, and rediscovered. I desire to hold nothing back, and I hope you won't either. Together, we will not only strengthen our trust in ourselves but also extend that trust outward—to our families, our communities, and the world beyond.

Here's my belief: by reclaiming trust within ourselves and nurturing it in others, we unlock a power that outpaces even the most advanced robot. Trust is, and will always be humanity's edge.

1

TURNING PROJECTIONS INTO POSSIBILITIES

"Everything that irritates us about others can lead us to an understanding of ourselves."

—Carl Jung

Growing up in Detroit, life presented its challenges. Don't get me wrong—Detroit is a city like no other, brimming with resilience and an indomitable spirit. Its rhythm, its culture, its people—everything about Detroit is unforgettable. I wouldn't trade my experiences there for anything. Even now, I return whenever I can, drawn back by the memories and the community that shaped me.

But as a child and teenager, navigating Detroit wasn't easy. It's a city steeped in history, a birthplace of public housing projects, and a stage for some of the harshest realities of poverty. It was a hub for ambition and survival, where drugs & violence made their mark and where opportunity often felt just out of reach. Over the years, Detroit has weathered decline and reinvention, but its essence remains strong. Despite the struggles, my love for this city is unwavering. It's where my story begins and where I learned to transform hardship into hope.

I grew up just a block from 8 Mile Road, the line dividing the suburbs from the inner city. My family was a working-class, single-parent household making ends meet, and I had to learn how to protect myself and my sister early on. I spent much of my time focused on my studies, talking to friends, playing baseball, basketball & football, and sitting on the street corners during the day where we dreamed about an impossible future. But as soon as the street lights came on, we had to be inside.

The dangers of the streets eventually seeped into who I was. There was internalized trauma—shaped by experiences I couldn't fully understand as a kid—and it impacted how we were raised. I took on the role of protector and sometimes provider for my sister. Uncertainty and dysfunctional family dynamics defined my teenage years. With an imbalance at home and harsh realities outside, my worldview became clouded by anger and frustration. My father's presence was less than desired due to the friction with my mother. While he was inconsistent, there were definitely major moments when he showed up when I needed it most. I was deemed the man of the house at the age of 5, where the weight of responsibility left little room for a normal childhood, forcing me to grow up faster than most.

This might be your back story, too. You might have grown up in a place where opportunities felt scarce, and hope seemed like a luxury. Maybe you were surrounded by challenges, and your family struggled just to make ends meet. If that's your story, I understand what it's like to carry the weight of survival on your shoulders at a young age. I know how easy it is to feel trapped by your circumstances, to let anger and frustration shape your path.

But there's something important I've learned along the way: your background doesn't have to define your future. The adversity you face can either hold you down or push you to rise above. The key is to begin to trust both yourself and other people. It's not easy at first. Trust isn't built overnight, but once you start to open up and rely on both your inner strength and the right people around you, you'll find that moving forward doesn't seem so impossible. In fact, it becomes the only option.

THE DAY I BEGAN TO LEARN TO TRUST

I still vividly remember one particular summer day when I was a teenager. I had just gone to the corner store and picked up something to drink and a snack. I was driving back home, minding my business, and as I turned down my street, I saw two of my friends running toward me. I could see the anxiety in their eyes. They didn't say much; they just jumped in my car and yelled, "Take us to the crib!" I didn't ask questions. I could feel the adrenaline rushing through their bodies, and I could feel my own pulse quicken. I didn't know where they were coming from, but whatever it was, it was serious.

After I dropped them off, I figured it was over. So I went on about my business, but it wasn't over.

Not even 10 minutes later, I was driving down a street when suddenly, out of nowhere, a Corvette and a van cornered me, blocking the road. I didn't recognize the cars, and I didn't know the people who jumped out of them either—two huge men armed with guns, their faces fixed with rage. My heart was pounding in my chest. These guys were serious, and I was completely unprepared.

One of them started yelling, "You jumped my cousin?" I was confused, still trying to process what was happening. "Who? I don't know what you're talking about," I was lost. But they didn't believe me. The situation was quickly spiraling out of control.

In a split second, I made a decision—out of panic, out of instinct—I punched one of the men in the mouth as hard as I could, then ran to get away. My body was moving faster than my mind could process, my heart was racing, and my breath was coming in short, desperate bursts. I heard gunshots behind me. They had put my car in drive, and it was rolling down the street, bullets ripping through it, the sound of metal being shredded by gunfire echoing in my ears.

I dove into some bushes, trying to make myself as small as possible, trying to disappear. My mind was spinning: *Why is this happening? What did I do?*

Eventually, the men drove off, but I wasn't safe yet. I ran to catch my car before it crashed into anything. My heart was still pounding, and I could feel my body shaking. My friend, who had been with me the whole time, jumped in the car, and I drove him home. But I wasn't going home. Not yet.

I went straight to a police officer I knew in the neighborhood, a woman who had always been fair to me. My voice was shaking as I told her what happened. "I didn't do anything this time, I swear. I've been trying to clean up my life. For real, you've got to believe me." She did. She knew I wasn't the same kid I used to be. So, she told me to call 9-1-1, and a couple of officers came by my house later that evening.

When the police finally arrived, I was standing outside with my mom, just trying to breathe, trying to convince myself that I was safe now. But safety was an illusion. The black officer looked at me, listened to my story, and seemed to believe me. But the white officer? He wasn't buying it. He knew me, or at least, he thought he did. He sneered at me, called me by my street name, "Smoke," and said, "I know who you are. I know what kind of people you hang around. I don't believe you, and we're not filing a report."

I felt deflated and couldn't control the rage building up inside me. "Fine," I said, "If you're not going to do anything, I will." I didn't even care anymore. I was done. I was ready to take matters into my own hands. I walked away from my house, not on the sidewalk but right in the middle of the street, like I didn't care if a car hit me or if those men came back for me. I was ready for anything. My whole life felt like it was crumbling, and I was powerless to stop it.

As I got closer to the house where it had all started, I could see a crowd of people outside. I wasn't thinking straight. I was in a daze, a rage-fueled, out-of-body kind of experience. I pulled out my gun and started walking straight toward the crowd.

Just as I was about to make a move, a man I didn't know at the time—Mr. Reed—grabbed me. As one of the fathers in the neighborhood, he had a commanding presence. "Son, don't do this. It's not worth it. You're a good kid." His voice broke through the chaos in my head, and suddenly, it was like time slowed down. I could hear one of the girls behind me crying. I could feel the weight of the gun in my hand. But it was Mr. Reed's words that hit me hardest. *You're a good kid. You don't have to do this.*

At that moment, everything inside me broke. The rage, the fear, the frustration—it all came crashing down. I started crying, my body shaking uncontrollably. I put the gun away, and Mr. Reed pulled me into his house. My mom came over, trying to comfort me, but it still stung. I was furious—not just at the situation, but at my mother for not believing me, my friends, and the world in everything that had pushed me to the brink.

The next day, I saw those friends again, the ones that the incident began with, and I was ready to fight. But then it hit me—I had to walk away. If I didn't, I'd be trapped in this cycle forever. I knew then that I had to leave, to distance myself from everything that could pull me back into that life.

I went away to college, but every time I came home, I'd visit Mr. Reed. He saved my life that night. If he hadn't stepped in, I don't know where I'd be today. Dead? In prison? Every time I drive past that house, I think about it. My mom still lives in the neighborhood, so I have to see it whenever I visit. It's a constant reminder of how close I came to throwing my whole life away.

Years later, when I started writing this book, I went to see Mr. Reed again. We laughed about that night, but deep down, I knew how much it meant. I hugged him and told him, "Thank you." His intervention didn't just save my life; it changed my entire path. And now, when I talk to people about overcoming their own struggles, I tell them about that night, about how one moment, one person, can make all the difference.

At the time, I didn't understand that my anger was mostly just me projecting. I didn't trust myself enough to know that my frustrations were really rooted in my own unhealed wounds and doubts. Instead of looking inward and addressing what was holding me back, I blamed everything and everyone around me.

IS PROJECTING JEOPARDIZING YOUR RELATIONSHIPS?

You may never have been in a situation where you almost killed someone, but chances are, you've found yourself seething with anger at times for no good reason other than you were projecting. Anger itself is not inherently bad—it's a natural human emotion that everyone experiences. It can be a healthy tool for setting boundaries, asserting ourselves, and protecting what we care about. But when left unchecked, anger can spiral out of control, and that's when it becomes dangerous. We might end up unleashing it on people who don't deserve it, sometimes even causing irreparable harm.

Think about the last time you found yourself furious over a seemingly insignificant issue—a frustrating drive, a workplace disagreement, or a miscommunication with a loved one. Now imagine that anger bubbling over and spilling out onto people who had no part in your frustration. This misplaced emotion can fracture relationships, fuel conflict, and leave you feeling isolated and misunderstood. While anger is natural, it's essential to recognize that how we express it can either build or destroy the connections we cherish.

The danger lies in the cycle of negativity that uncontrolled anger creates. Every time we lash out at someone who doesn't deserve it, we perpetuate a sense of hostility and resentment. This ongoing pattern erodes trust, disrupts communication, and makes it harder to maintain healthy relationships. And when we project our anger onto others, we ignore the root cause of our frustrations, allowing the destructive cycle to continue. Recognizing these patterns is the first step in breaking free from them.

I had to face a harsh truth about myself: a lot of my anger was really a projection of my own unresolved insecurities. One particular instance stands out—a work project where I found myself snapping at my team for even the smallest mistakes. The tension in the office was palpable. It wasn't until a trusted colleague pulled me aside and asked if I was okay that I took a moment to reflect. That conversation marked the beginning of my journey toward self-awareness.

Through deep introspection, I realized that the anger I directed at others was rooted in my own fear and feelings of inadequacy. I was projecting my internal chaos onto innocent people, blaming them for the turmoil I hadn't confronted in myself. This realization was both painful and liberating. By acknowledging my inner struggles, I found healthier ways to manage my anger and improve my relationships.

PROJECTION AS A DEFENSE MECHANISM

Researchers suggest that projection is a defense mechanism—an unconscious way of shielding ourselves from painful emotions like guilt, shame, or fear. It's a mental escape route, a way to deflect discomfort by shifting our emotions onto others. And while projection may offer temporary relief, it ultimately prevents us from confronting the issues within ourselves.

Think about it: when you project, you're making someone else responsible for your emotions. Say you feel insecure about your abilities at work, and instead of confronting those feelings, you start criticizing others for their perceived incompetence. This doesn't solve your problem—it just masks it, unfairly burdening those around you with your unresolved issues. Projection keeps us stuck in a cycle of avoidance, preventing personal growth and healing.

When projection is used to displace anger, the damage is even more profound. Instead of addressing the real source of our emotions, we lash out at others, sowing discord and confusion. Hurtful words are exchanged, trust is broken, and relationships are strained. In the aftermath, we feel both misunderstood and responsible for the fallout. Projection distorts reality, making it seem as though the problem lies outside us when, in fact, it's something we need to face internally.

But here's the good news: You don't have to live like this. The key to breaking the cycle of projection lies in self-awareness. By recognizing when we're projecting, we can begin to take responsibility for our emotions and start the journey of personal growth. This will also prevent you from letting one bad moment cost you your entire life.

BREAKING FREE FROM THE CYCLE

When I was younger, I was a master at projecting my frustrations and insecurities onto others. But with the help of friends, mentors, and therapy, I've learned how to stop. And if someone like me—someone who once lived with walls built by fear and defense mechanisms—can break free, so can you.

The first step is recognizing when you're projecting. This wasn't easy for me. At first, I didn't even realize I was displacing my issues onto others. But with time, I learned to pay attention to my emotional reactions, especially in moments of anger or frustration. I started asking myself: "Is that what really happened?" and "What's really bothering me?" These simple question helped me uncover the deeper emotions I had been ignoring—feelings of fear, inadequacy, and self-doubt. It became my tool for self-reflection, giving me the space to step back before reacting.

Identifying emotional triggers is essential. Think about a time when you got angry over something small—a mistake at work or an offhand comment from a friend. For me, it was an error at work that led to an explosive reaction. But after reflecting, I realized it wasn't the mistake that triggered me. It was my own fear of failure and inadequacy. By identifying the real cause of my anger, I was able to address it directly rather than projecting it onto someone else.

Mindfulness has been another crucial tool in my journey. By practicing mindfulness, we learn to pause and observe our emotions without immediately reacting to them. I remember a heated conversation with a family member where I could feel my anger rising. Instead of responding with frustration, I took a moment to breathe and reflect. That pause allowed me to approach the situation with more understanding and less reactivity.

Mindfulness helps us break the automatic patterns that lead to projection. It teaches us to respond thoughtfully, not impulsively. And with practice, we begin to replace old, reactive habits with healthier, more constructive responses.

THE POWER OF SELF-TRUST

Here's the bottom line: our emotions are our own responsibility. No one else is responsible for how we feel or how we respond to situations. By taking ownership of our emotions, we stop blaming others and start seeing people and situations for what they truly are—rather than through the lens of our insecurities.

As I learned to stop projecting, I found that I trusted myself more deeply. I trusted my intuition, my judgment, and my ability to navigate life's challenges with grace. And as my self-trust grew, so did my ability to trust others. I was no longer clouded by fear or insecurity, and my relationships became more authentic and grounded in mutual respect.

Remember, you have the power within you to stop projecting. It requires work, but it's worth it. As Michael Jordan wisely said, "Some people want it to happen, some wish it would happen, and others make it happen." Are you ready to make it happen?

2

VULNERABILITY IS POWER

"Vulnerability is the birthplace of innovation, creativity, and change."

—Brené Brown

As a young boy, my environment was unforgiving—a relentless trial where survival depended on my ability to figure things out on my own. The absence of a strong foundation at home left a void that chaos eagerly filled, accompanied by instability and a constant undercurrent of fear. In the absence of support and guidance, I was forced to grow up fast, navigating the harsh realities of my neighborhood with a resilience born out of necessity.

Even at an early age, I lived in a perpetual state of vigilance. I was always alert, scanning my surroundings for danger lurking around the corner. Every day was a battle, and in a place like that, even a hint of vulnerability could be seen as an invitation to exploit. In the inner-city, vulnerability wasn't just frowned upon; it was dangerous. It was a perceived weakness—a crack in the armor that could invite harm. To survive, I had to build my own armor, layering it piece by piece to shield myself from the blows life seemed determined to deliver.

This armor, a tough exterior forged by experience, became my constant companion. By the time I was eight, I had developed an emotional fortitude that acted as both sword and shield. I learned to wear a brave face like a badge of honor, even when fear or pain clawed at me from within. My defense mechanism worked—it allowed me to navigate the treacherous terrain of my neighborhood without succumbing to despair. But it came at a cost. The armor, while protective, was also heavy.

As a Black boy—and later, a Black man—this burden was compounded by the weight of societal expectations. There was an unspoken rule that Black men had to be unyielding pillars of strength, immune to pain, and impervious to weakness. To deviate from this narrative was to risk judgment, ridicule, and rejection—not just from society but sometimes even from those within our own communities. Vulnerability was not an option; it was a liability.

For decades, I lived imprisoned by my own armor. It protected me, yes, but it also kept me isolated, locking away my authentic self. I struggled to connect deeply with others because the walls I built to keep danger out also kept love, trust, and understanding at bay. My inability to let anyone in left me feeling profoundly alone despite the image of strength I had worked so hard to project.

When I left for college in 1997, I carried this survival mindset with me. The same armor that had kept me safe as a child became a hindrance in my adult life. Trusting others felt like an insurmountable challenge; I had never been taught how to rely on anyone but myself. I worked tirelessly to prove my worth, driven by an unspoken fear of failure and rejection.

And though my relentless effort led to accomplishments, it also left me emotionally drained.

Asking for help felt foreign—almost dangerous. I had been conditioned to equate vulnerability with weakness, and so I fought invisible battles in silence, unwilling to show the world the weight I carried. While others seemed to savor the journey, I was still bracing for a fight, living as though the ground beneath me could vanish at any moment. The habits that had once kept me safe were now barriers to my growth, my happiness, and my ability to truly live.

But life has a way of teaching us what we most need to learn. It wasn't until much later that I realized the power of vulnerability—the courage it takes to lay down your armor and show the world who you really are. It's not easy to unlearn survival, but in doing so, I discovered a freedom I never thought possible.

Let me share a story that illustrates this transformation, a moment when I began to dismantle the walls that had both protected and confined me. It was through this journey that I learned the profound strength found in vulnerability—and how embracing it changed my life forever.

In 2008, the automotive industry was in disarray. The economy had just collapsed, and jobs were scarce. General Motors experienced its infamous Black Tuesday, with mass layoffs and an uncertain future. Amidst this chaos, I felt fortunate to have a job at GM, working on the groundbreaking Chevrolet Chevy Volt, an electric vehicle that was seen as a beacon of hope during tough times. I was hired based on my successful experience working on the Hummer H3, a mid-size SUV that was produced by General Motors under the Hummer brand from 2005 to 2010. Designed to provide the rugged off-road capabilities of its larger siblings, the H3 offered a more practical size for everyday use while still maintaining the brand's distinctive military-inspired aesthetics. I was instrumental in the manufacturing operations process automation development of the robots that assembled the body of the H3.

So, the Group Director assigned me to the Volt project as the Lead Robotics Engineer. One day, I walked into a meeting where the team for the electric car was being introduced. As a well-known and respected robotics engineer, I was ready to contribute. A white gentleman I had never met before was there, looking around the room as the introductions were made.

"Who's the Robot Engineer?" he asked, scanning the faces in the room.

One of my colleagues pointed to me and said, "You're sitting right next to him."

He chuckled and shook his head. "No, seriously, who's the Lead Robot Engineer?"

Before I could respond, another colleague who knew my work spoke up from across the table. "If Terrence is leading, you're in good hands. Don't worry about anything. He's going to make sure everything is done properly."

The room fell silent for a moment. It was an awkward but revealing experience. Despite my accomplishments, there was still a level of skepticism and a lack of respect for my capabilities. It was a stark reminder of the challenges I faced throughout my career. Even with numerous successes under my belt, my presence in such a role was often questioned. And for one reason only: I'm a black man.

Reflecting on my journey, I realized that it wasn't just about that one incident. From the start of my career and even today, it's rare to see someone like me in the room, especially from an engineering and robotics perspective. Seeing a black person in an important role, such as the Lead Robotics Engineer was uncommon and, unfortunately, still is.

Why do I share this story with you?

This example highlights how difficult it is to become vulnerable when your competence and achievements are constantly questioned. For me, vulnerability meant risking being seen as weak or incompetent in an industry where I already faced enough bias. Each time I had to prove myself over and over again, it reinforced the need to maintain a tough exterior, further distancing me from showing any vulnerability. Admitting any uncertainty or seeking help could be easily misconstrued as a lack of ability rather than a normal part of the learning process.

The emotional toll of continuously having to defend my position and capabilities made it even harder to open up and show my true self. When the very essence of who you are—a black man in a predominantly white field—is frequently challenged, it creates an additional layer of pressure to conform to the image of unwavering strength and infallibility. This, in turn, stifles personal growth and prevents the development of deeper, more authentic connections—both professionally and personally. It becomes a vicious cycle where the fear of being vulnerable only exacerbates the feelings of isolation and doubt.

What about you? Do you also feel like you can't be vulnerable like you have to put on a face? This is something not only black men (and women) feel. I think many of us feel pressured to maintain a facade of strength and composure, hiding our true emotions and struggles behind a mask. Sometimes, it feels like showing any sign of vulnerability would expose us to judgment, criticism, or even exploitation. This pressure can be overwhelming, forcing us to suppress our feelings and present a version of ourselves that aligns with societal expectations.

Whether it's in our personal relationships, at work, or in social settings, the fear of being seen as weak or inadequate often leads us to conceal our true selves. This is exhausting! It isolates us and prevents us from forming genuine connections and experiencing personal growth.

Vulnerability is often associated with weakness, fragility, and insecurity. I once believed that showing vulnerability was akin to admitting defeat, exposing myself to criticism, or displaying a lack of confidence. As a result, I went to great lengths to avoid being vulnerable, putting up emotional walls, and adopting a facade of invincibility. I feared that vulnerability would make me appear weak and exposed, leaving me open to judgment and rejection. I wore a mask. But let me tell you, that mask was heavy, and it kept me from experiencing the true depth of human connection.

However, I have ultimately discovered that vulnerability can be a profound source of strength, resilience, and personal growth. It takes immense courage to be vulnerable, to open up and to share my true self with others. When I've embraced vulnerability, I'm seen more authentically by other people, and I've fostered deeper and more trust-filled connections. By acknowledging my imperfections and insecurities, I pave the way for genuine relationships and meaningful interactions. This realization has transformed my life, showing me that true strength lies in the courage to be vulnerable.

I want to shift your perspective on vulnerability. Vulnerability isn't something to be avoided or suppressed. It's a powerful tool for personal development and transformation. By embracing it, we can cultivate a richer, more fulfilling life marked by more authentic connections.

WHAT IS VULNERABILITY?

Vulnerability is often misunderstood. According to the Merriam-Webster Dictionary, it means "capable of being attacked or wounded." But in the realm of human connection, vulnerability is so much more. It's the act of being open, honest, and transparent with ourselves—allowing our emotions, thoughts, and experiences to be seen by others. It's a raw expression of trust in ourselves and in the people around us. Vulnerability sounds like truth and looks like courage.

It's not about exposing every detail to just anyone, nor is it about seeking sympathy. True vulnerability is about shedding the layers that mask our fears, limitations, and imperfections. It's about showing up as we truly are—unfiltered and unapologetically human. When we embrace this authenticity, we forge deeper connections that are grounded in trust, empathy, and mutual understanding.

Now, you might be asking yourself: *Why embrace vulnerability? What could possibly be gained from exposing the most fragile parts of myself?* Let me paint a picture for you. Imagine a room full of people, each one armored with facades—protecting themselves from the world and from each other. Then, you decide to take off your armor. At first, it feels terrifying, like you're standing naked before the world. But here's the miracle: as you let down your guard, others begin to do the same. Vulnerability invites vulnerability. It creates a space where true connection thrives, where relationships move beyond surface-level exchanges to something deeper, something more real.

In this space, you don't see each other through the lens of perfection but through the shared humanity that connects us all. And in this raw, authentic exchange, relationships are no longer fragile—they are built on trust and understanding.

Vulnerability is not just about connection with others. It's also a powerful engine for personal growth. Stepping into vulnerability forces us out of our comfort zones, challenging us to take risks and try new things. With every moment of openness, we learn more about ourselves and grow stronger. We become more adaptable, more resilient, and more capable of facing life's challenges.

Healing begins with vulnerability. When we allow ourselves to truly feel—whether it's joy, pain, sadness, or fear—we begin the process of emotional healing. Ignoring or suppressing our emotions only keeps us stuck. But when we open up, we make space for release, growth, and transformation. In embracing our emotional truth, we become more authentic and more relatable. We no longer feel burdened by the weight of unspoken fears or hidden wounds, and our lives take on a richness that only comes from living fully.

Vulnerability also nurtures empathy. By sharing our struggles, we remind others that they are not alone. We create bridges of understanding and compassion, breaking down walls of isolation. In this space, differences fade away, and the shared experience of being human takes center stage.

OVERCOMING THE FEAR OF VULNERABILITY

Now, you may be thinking, *this all sounds beautiful, but how do I begin?* The fear of being vulnerable is real. It's normal to be scared of opening up, especially if you've been hurt in the past. But I promise you this: it's worth it. And it's a journey you don't have to take all at once.

Start small. You don't need to bear your soul to everyone right away. Begin with a single, simple act of openness—maybe sharing a thought or feeling with a trusted friend, a family member, or even a mentor. These small steps are like muscle-building exercises for your vulnerability. Every time you speak from the heart, even in the tiniest way, you gain strength.

You might feel exposed at first, but here's what you'll discover: vulnerability fosters intimacy. It creates deeper bonds with the people who matter most to you. It lightens the load of emotional burden, making it easier to be yourself. So, don't rush the process. Celebrate every small victory, no matter how small it feels. These moments build momentum, and before you know it, your capacity for vulnerability will expand.

Next, embrace your imperfections. Vulnerability is not about being flawless—it's about being real. It's about showing up as your true self, flaws and all. When you accept yourself fully, without judgment, you open the door for others to do the same. Let go of perfectionism, and allow yourself the freedom to be human. It's in this space of self-acceptance that vulnerability becomes not just a practice but a superpower.

THE POWER OF MINDSET

Changing how you view vulnerability is key to embracing it. You might have negative beliefs that vulnerability is a weakness or that it will lead to rejection. But those beliefs are based on fear, not truth. Challenge these beliefs. Ask yourself: *What if a vulnerability is not a risk but an opportunity?*

When you begin to reframe vulnerability as a strength, you'll notice a shift. Vulnerability is the gateway to deeper connections, to growth, and to breakthroughs. It allows you to become more aligned with your authentic self, which is the foundation of your greatest potential.

SUPPORT AND GUIDANCE

You don't have to face vulnerability alone. Seeking guidance from a therapist, coach, or trusted mentor can be a game-changer. These professionals can help you navigate your fears, reshape negative beliefs, and develop the tools you need to thrive in vulnerability. Imagine working with someone who believes in your potential and supports you in stepping into your full, authentic self.

A therapist or coach can be the bridge to a richer, more fulfilling life—one where vulnerability is not a burden but a source of strength, healing, and empowerment.

So, I'll leave you with this challenge: take the first step. As coach Tony Dungy wisely says, *"Avoidance doesn't solve anything; it merely serves as a temporary salve."* Don't wait for the "perfect moment"—now is the time to begin. Vulnerability is not just a practice; it's a key to unlocking freedom, connection, and personal growth.

Take off your armor. Step into the light. Let your true self shine. Remember, the real strength is in the willingness to be open, to be honest, and to be yourself.

3

LOVE + ACCEPTANCE = TRUST

"If you truly love someone, you must be willing to accept them as they are, without expecting them to change, and trust that the love between you will allow you both to grow."

—Jack Kornfield

Growing up in Detroit, I can't say I truly knew what love was. Love wasn't something we talked about or even really felt in the same way I'd hear others describe it later in life. The only life I knew was staying strong and protecting yourself. Love, if it was there at all, was tough, guarded, and hidden beneath layers of resilience and grit. The warmth, the openness, and the understanding that I would come to know as love later—that was something I had to find for myself over time.

When you don't feel loved, trust becomes a difficult concept to grasp. That's because trust is rooted in a sense of safety, in the assurance that someone cares for you and has your best interests at heart. But without that foundation of love, there's nothing solid to build on. It's like trying to walk on quicksand—you're hesitant unsure, and every step feels unstable. Instead of trust, you develop walls, defenses meant to protect you from the uncertainty and vulnerability that come with relying on someone else. You learn to rely on yourself because, without love, trusting others feels like a risk you can't afford to take.

Fortunately, amidst all the chaos and uncertainty, there was one person in my life who truly saw me—saw past the rough edges, the guarded demeanor, and the defenses I had learned to wear. Her name was Mrs. Jennings, and she will always hold a special place in my heart. She was my neighbor from down my block who was like a mother to me, but she was more than that. She was a constant presence in my unstable life; she was my adult best friend and the first person I would want to tell good news to even when I had a new girlfriend.

I'll never forget the day she asked if I'd help look after her two sons after school, Eric and Brandon. It seemed like a small thing at the time, but to me, it felt like she was offering me a chance to display a side not many had seen and be part of something more than just survival. So, I spent several years with her sons, teaching them how to play video games, shoot hoops, and help them with their homework.

Frankly, I was surprised she trusted me with her children. She didn't see me as just another kid from the block. She saw me as someone with potential, someone worthy of responsibility and trust. She believed in me, even when I didn't yet believe in myself. Mrs. Jennings's simple request—to help care for Eric and Brandon—became one of the most significant moments of my life. It was the first time I felt seen and valued; I knew there was nothing to worry about when she was around. She was my model of what a friend, mother, and wife should be as I grew forward in my future. I didn't fully realize this at the time; it was more of a subconscious feeling. Later, however, I realized the full impact.

But that never discounted the trauma I experienced in my childhood; when you've had things taken from you—things you've worked hard for, things you've built with your own hands—you learn to be guarded. You learn to protect yourself and keep your defenses high. That's exactly what I did for most of my life. I was guarded, off-putting even, with body language that probably made others uncomfortable. On the surface, people saw a confident, nice guy, but they couldn't shake the feeling that I was hiding something. In truth, I was. I was hiding myself. Other than Mrs. Jennings, there weren't many other people who displayed that level of trust in me.

For many years, I hid who I truly was. I carried my past in a safe place, a place I didn't let anyone near. When I left for college, I found myself in a new world. Everyone around me seemed to come from what I believed to be perfect backgrounds—families that loved them and friends that supported them. They hadn't grown up around drugs, violence, or juvenile detention centers. For them, those things were foreign concepts. For me, they were everyday life.

So, I tried to blend in. I kept my stories to myself, afraid of what people might think if they knew the truth. But over time, I began to realize something profound. It was those very stories that made me who I was. Those experiences, those struggles, were the source of my strength and resilience. They were the reason people could see the beauty in me as an individual. I started to open up to share my past, and I found that people were inspired by it. They admired me for what I had overcome.

Today, I've learned to lean into trust. It starts with trusting myself and knowing that it's okay to be me. It's okay to open up and let others in. After all, who can take advantage of you when you've got God protecting you?

One memory stands out to me, a pivotal moment in my journey of learning to trust. A few years ago, I was launching my nonprofit organization, Illuminate STEM. But the problem was I didn't know the first thing about how to do that. So, I reached out to a friend for help. She connected me with an attorney named William Taylor, Esq. From the moment we met, we hit it off as if I had known him for years. I wanted (and needed) an attorney because I was so used to people trying to take things from me. I was always in defense mode, trying to protect what was mine— I sometimes still struggle with this, even today.

However, something incredible happened when I met William. I told him what I needed, and he quickly shared that he had the experience to deliver on my request. As we wrapped up our business discussion, we started talking on a personal level. The next moment, he says, "Southern? That's a unique last name. Do you know Noceeba Southern?". I replied that it was my cousin. The familiarity took the conversation to the next level. We discovered that we were both from Detroit, grew up in the same neighborhood, attended the same high school in Detroit, and even had the same nickname, "Smoke." Before you know it, we were debating who was the G.O.A.T, Jordan vs. Lebron. You already know who I ride with. We shared so many common experiences that, before I knew it, I felt like I had met my best friend. We became close, and he served as a big brother to me. This connection produced multiple business ideas, and for years, he and his wife gave me invaluable advice on relationships and life.

At the same time, there were many things he didn't know about me since I trusted him and needed a listening ear. I sat in his office as we wrapped up our business talk, wondering just how much to divulge. To open up to this man about who

I was and what I was about? To share about my childhood and my struggles? Maybe even my roots are on the streets of Detroit? I don't know why, but I chose to open up. Then, the conversation really started moving. In a sense, it continued on for many years afterward—William became one of my most trusted confidants.

This experience (and William himself) taught me a valuable lesson. Sometimes, you have to put some skin in the game. I couldn't keep guarding my heart and expect to build meaningful relationships. I had to open up, trust others, and let go of the fear that my past would define my future.

William passed away on March 1, 2020, just prior to what we called COVID-19 10 days later. It was one of the most difficult losses I have ever experienced, and it momentarily halted all of my progress. But then I was reminded about the importance of finishing what you start by a friend who framed a picture of the last picture William and I took to motivate me to the finish line. So, the mission of our work together continues, and I am committed to not letting him down as he watches from afar.

THE TRUST FORMULA

Trust is the bedrock of any healthy relationship. It's the invisible thread that weaves together the fabric of our connections—whether with partners, family, friends, or colleagues. Trust allows us to feel safe, secure, and vulnerable with those we care about. Yet, let's face it: building and maintaining trust can be one of the hardest things to do, especially when past wounds of betrayal, disappointment, or hurt linger in the shadows of our hearts. So, how do we lay the foundation for trust in our lives? The answer lies in two powerful pillars: **love** and **acceptance**. Imagine trying to construct a house on unsteady ground. No matter how beautiful the structure, it won't stand for long. The same is true for relationships. Without the solid grounding of love and acceptance, trust wavers, cracks, and ultimately collapses.

LOVE: THE FIRST PILLAR

When I speak of love, I'm not limiting it to the romantic kind. Love is far more expansive. It embodies compassion, empathy, and genuine kindness. Love means truly seeing another person—their struggles, their joys, and their worth—and choosing to honor their humanity. When we love someone, we validate their feelings and experiences. This validation creates a sanctuary, a safe space where they feel seen, heard, and valued. And here's the beautiful thing: when someone feels valued, they're more likely to open up, be vulnerable, and trust. It's a virtuous cycle. This truth came alive for me through William and Mrs. Jennings. Their kindness and unwavering belief in me taught me how transformative love can be. They didn't just teach me to trust them—they helped me trust myself again.

ACCEPTANCE: THE COMPANION PILLAR

Love without acceptance is incomplete. To accept someone is to embrace them in their entirety—their strengths, quirks, and flaws. Acceptance is saying, *"I see who you are, and I choose you anyway."* This kind of radical acceptance creates freedom. It frees us to be our true selves, unburdened by the fear of judgment. And in that space, trust flourishes. Think about it:

how can trust exist if you're constantly worried about being criticized or rejected? Acceptance isn't about ignoring imperfections; it's about holding space for someone's humanity while nurturing the connection you share.

LOVE + ACCEPTANCE = THE CATALYST FOR HEALING

Here's where love and acceptance become transformative: they help us move beyond the scars of betrayal and hurt. If you've ever been betrayed, you know the emotional toll it takes. For some, it feels like a permanent wound. But love and acceptance offer a bridge to healing. When we feel genuinely loved and accepted, we find the strength to forgive—not to erase the past, but to reclaim our future. Trust can be rebuilt, piece by piece, on the foundation of unconditional care. This process isn't just for the betrayed; it strengthens the bond between partners, friends, or family members. When love and acceptance are mutual, they create a deeper sense of connection. We invest more in the relationship, weather challenges together, and grow in trust.

BUILDING TRUST THROUGH ACTION

Trust doesn't grow in a vacuum. It's cultivated through intentional actions. Here are some practical ways to nurture trust through love and acceptance:

PRACTICE ACTIVE LISTENING

When someone shares with you, give them your undivided attention. Put down your phone, make eye contact, and truly listen—not just to their words, but to their emotions and unspoken cues. Active listening shows that you value their thoughts and feelings, reinforcing their sense of trust in you.

EXPRESS GRATITUDE REGULARLY

A simple "thank you" can have a profound impact. Acknowledging someone's efforts shows that you don't take them for granted. Gratitude creates a ripple effect, fostering positivity and trust within the relationship.

CULTIVATE EMPATHY AND FORGIVENESS

Empathy is about stepping into someone else's shoes, even when it's uncomfortable. It says, "I see your pain, and I'm here for you." Paired with forgiveness, empathy becomes a powerful force for healing. Forgiveness isn't about excusing harmful behavior; it's about releasing resentment so trust can be rebuilt.

DEMONSTRATE CONSISTENCY

Trust thrives on reliability. Show up when you say you will. Follow through on your commitments. Small, consistent actions are the building blocks of enduring trust.

TRUST IN ACTION

Finally, don't underestimate the power of showing trust in others. Be like Mrs. Jennings. Someone out there needs to feel your love, respect, and belief in them. Imagine the ripple effect that trust could have on their life. The truth is trust isn't just the glue that holds relationships together; it's the catalyst for growth, healing, and transformation. Through love and acceptance, we can strengthen this bond and create relationships that are not just enduring but deeply fulfilling. So take the first step. Build a foundation of trust by embracing love and acceptance in all its forms. You might just change someone's life—including your own.

4

BREAK OUT OF YOUR BOX

"Change begins at the end of your comfort zone."

—Roy T. Bennett

'm most comfortable living outside the box.

In fact, I'm so used to taking the road less traveled that I struggle to answer people's questions about how I do this and what I've learned from it. To me, it's simply how I view the world. I've never been one to follow the crowd blindly. When ninety-nine people are heading in one direction, I'm the one standing still, looking for an alternative path. I want to be one of the one percenters—the few who dare to explore the other side before making a decision.

I remember an experience at the airport recently. I had just walked off a plane and was headed to baggage claim. Everyone was following the person in front of them—you know how it goes. It's easier to just do what everyone else is doing than try to figure out, all on your own, where you need to go.

As we all walked toward two sets of automated doors—one on the left, the other on the right—I noticed something peculiar. Everyone who'd been on my plane was funneling through the door on the left. It was a big crowd, and everyone had to slow down to get through this one door. The movement came to a total standstill. Imagine a wide river being forced through a small ravine, water pooling into a wide lake behind it.

All the while, the door on the right remained unused—almost like it was invisible. This struck me as odd. Was the door on the left more inviting because it was already open? Did people just follow the crowd without questioning why? Wouldn't using both doors make things move faster?

As it often does, my curiosity got the best of me. I walked toward the unused door on the right. As I approached, it opened effortlessly, almost as if it had been eagerly waiting for someone to show up. I walked through and passed everyone in the crowd. I looked back over my shoulder and noticed that dozens of others began to follow my lead. The crowd dissipated, and we all got to our homes (or our hotels) a bit quicker that day.

Sure, this was a small moment. Nothing groundbreaking. But the experience perfectly encapsulates how I approach life. The fact is, we human beings often follow the path that's already been tread for the simple reason that it's already there. We don't question it; we don't think about it. We do what seems easiest. But much of the time, there's an equally viable—or even better—path just steps away. It takes just one pioneering person who believes in himself to break the mold and carve a new and better way forward.

I've always been someone who goes against the grain. I attribute this to my deep curiosity. In many ways, I was born with it—a curiosity that sets me apart and makes me see the world differently. Ever heard of the Dilbert comic? A Dilbert cartoon comes to mind. It talks about "the knack"—that innate curiosity that drives people to become engineers, to take things apart and see what's going on inside. I'm that kind of person. I thrive on going down the rabbit hole, whether it's about politics, engineering, innovation, religion, or relationships. I don't just want to see the surface—I want to understand the inner workings, the mechanisms that make things tick.

This curiosity keeps me from becoming what I fear most: a robot. That's ironic, maybe, because robotics is what I do. I'm a robotics engineer. But sometimes, I wonder who the real robots are—are they the machines, or are they us? We're all programmed, in one way or another, to think a certain way, to follow certain paths. But I've always resisted that programming. I've made a conscious decision to live outside the box, forge my own path, and control my own mindset.

In a world where so many are content to follow, I choose to break out of my box—even if it means walking through a door that no one else sees.

BE YOUR BIGGEST FAN

There's a saying: *"If you don't stand for something, you'll fall for anything."* At the heart of standing firm for what you believe in lies the ability to trust yourself. It's not just about being confident in your convictions but about having the courage to defend them, the resilience to endure opposition, and the authenticity to stay true to your core values. Trusting yourself is the gateway to living with purpose and integrity, and it's the first step toward a life that is both empowered and meaningful.

SELF-TRUST FUELS CONFIDENCE

Trusting yourself is the foundation of confidence. When you trust yourself, you trust your decisions, your instincts, and your ability to navigate life's challenges. This belief in yourself isn't just a fleeting feeling; it's a deep, rooted conviction that you can handle whatever life throws at you—even when it pushes you out of your comfort zone. Confidence born from self-trust isn't arrogance; it's a quiet assurance that you are enough. You can be uncertain and still move forward, and that is the power of self-trust.

RESILIENCE: THE POWER TO RISE AGAIN

Trusting yourself also builds resilience. Life will inevitably throw curveballs—setbacks, failures, and obstacles that feel insurmountable at times. But when you trust yourself, you see these challenges as opportunities for growth. You don't crumble under the weight of adversity. Instead, you rise. You grow stronger, smarter, and more determined with each obstacle you overcome. Every setback is merely a stepping stone toward success, and every small victory strengthens your resolve.

AUTHENTICITY: THE COURAGE TO BE YOU

Beyond confidence and resilience, self-trust leads to authenticity. When you trust yourself, you stop trying to fit into others' molds or seek validation from external sources. You stand in your truth unapologetically, no matter the pressure to conform. Authenticity means embracing your quirks, your passions, and your imperfections. It's a radical act of self-acceptance in a world that often rewards the opposite. But when you live authentically, you attract the right opportunities, people, and experiences—ones that resonate with the true you. And that is where genuine connection happens.

UNLEASH YOUR INNER GREATNESS

Self-trust is the foundation of your greatness, not just a nice-to-have trait. When you trust yourself, you unlock a limitless power within you. You walk taller, speak with more conviction, and act with purpose. Your presence becomes magnetic, and your words carry weight. When you trust yourself, you become unstoppable. The challenges that once seemed daunting now feel like opportunities. The voice of doubt is drowned out by the sound of your own self-belief. You are a force.

THE JOURNEY TO TRUST YOURSELF

But let's be real: trusting yourself is no easy feat. It's a journey—a process that involves confronting fears, doubts, and the voices of inner criticism that can be deafening. That voice—the one that tells you you're not good enough, that you can't do it—will always be there, but it doesn't have to control you. To trust yourself is to challenge that voice every single day and replace it with affirmations of your capability, your worth, and your right to pursue your dreams.

EMBRACE FAILURES AS STEPPING STONES

Along the way, failure is inevitable. It's not a matter of if you will fail, but when. But when you trust yourself, you learn to see failure not as a roadblock but as part of the journey. It's not a setback but a lesson. Failures become opportunities for growth. You get back up. You get stronger. You get wiser. Every time you fall, you rise higher.

LIVING AUTHENTICALLY IN A WORLD THAT WANTS TO MOLD YOU

In a world that often pressures you to be someone else, living authentically is nothing short of revolutionary. It's a refusal to be anything less than your true self, no matter the consequences. It's about standing proud of your uniqueness, regardless of whether the world around you understands it. But when you embrace your authenticity, you create deeper, more meaningful connections with the people around you— people who appreciate the real you and who inspire you to become an even better version of yourself.

THE RIPPLE EFFECT OF TRUST

When you stand for what you believe in, you ignite a ripple effect. Your actions inspire others to do the same. Your courage becomes contagious. You become a beacon of strength and integrity, showing the world that it's possible to live with conviction, to fight for what matters, and to make an impact. In a world that sometimes feels passive or indifferent, your voice can spark change. Your example can catalyze a movement. The more you stand in your truth, the more you inspire others to stand in theirs.

BUILDING THE TRUST TO FIGHT FOR WHAT MATTERS

So, how do you build this self-trust, the kind that empowers you to stand up for what you care about?

1. **Identify Your Core Values:** Take the time to reflect on what truly matters to you. What do you stand for? What do you care about deeply? Knowing your values gives you clarity and purpose. Without this self-awareness, it's impossible to stand firm in the face of opposition.

2. **Set Boundaries:** Protect your beliefs and values by establishing clear boundaries. Communicate them confidently, and don't allow others to undermine your integrity. Boundaries act as a shield that protects your focus, energy, and dreams.

3. **Practice Self-Compassion:** Nobody is perfect, and that includes you. Self-trust isn't about being flawless; it's about being kind to yourself through mistakes and setbacks. It's about understanding that every failure is a lesson, not a defeat. Trusting yourself means embracing your imperfections and being patient with your growth.

4. **Cultivate a Supportive Network:** Surround yourself with people who believe in you. Build a community of like-minded individuals who encourage you, challenge you, and help you stay focused on your goals.

A solid support network amplifies your strength and resilience.

5. **Focus on the Process:** The road to self-trust isn't about a singular destination; it's about the journey. Celebrate progress, not just outcomes. Each step, no matter how small, is a victory. Embrace the lessons of failure and keep moving forward. Trusting yourself is a continuous process of growth.

Trusting yourself and standing up for your values are transformative acts of courage and self-empowerment. When you build this trust, you step into your authentic power, and you can begin to shape the world around you. Trust yourself—because the world needs your unique strength, your voice, and your vision. Stand tall, live with purpose, and never forget: you are your greatest ally in this journey.

5

DON'T LOOK BACK

"Don't ever stop. Keep going.
If you want a taste of freedom, keep going."

—Harriet Tubman

The temptation to look back can be as intoxicating as it is paralyzing. A glance over the shoulder, whether born of curiosity, doubt, or regret, can tether us to a past that no longer serves us. Memories of what was, or fantasies of what could have been, often cloud our ability to fully embrace what lies ahead. But the truth is, looking back does little to change the past. Instead, it diverts our focus and slows our momentum, leaving us stuck in moments we cannot rewrite.

Harriet Tubman's words remind us of the unyielding determination required to pursue freedom—freedom from fear, from failure, and from the illusions that keep us anchored in yesterday. This chapter challenges you to confront the urge to revisit old chapters of your life and instead channel your energy into moving forward with purpose and clarity.

Life's journey isn't meant to be navigated with one foot in the past. Each step forward demands courage, not just to face the unknown but to release the weight of what once was. Whether it's the sting of a mistake, the ache of a missed opportunity, or the echo of lingering doubts, these are mere distractions, shadows on the road to becoming your truest self.

To walk boldly into the future, you must make peace with the past. Accept it for what it taught you, honor the lessons it offered, and then set it down. Looking back, you may feel safe, but safety is not the same as growth. Growth requires trust—trust in the path before you, trust in your ability to adapt, and trust that each forward step will bring you closer to fulfillment.

The power of not looking back lies in its ability to sharpen your vision for what's ahead. It's about quieting the noise, silencing the doubts, and choosing to believe in the possibility of what's to come. The road forward may not always be smooth, but every stumble, every twist, and every turn has a purpose—to propel you toward a future only you can create.

So, what's holding you back? What's keeping your eyes on the rearview mirror instead of the horizon? This is your moment to decide: Will you let the past define you, or will you take that first step into a future filled with endless possibilities?

The choice is yours. Don't look back. Keep going.

I'm grateful to have learned this lesson, but I'll admit it took me a while to grasp it. To help others understand what I mean, I take them through a team-building exercise. This team-building exercise is simple but incredibly powerful. Imagine a door at the far end of the room—just an ordinary door, the kind you'd walk through without a second thought. But in this exercise, it becomes a test of focus, resilience, and the ability to move forward without distraction.

Here's how it begins. We ask one team member to walk from one side of the room, across the threshold of the door, and back. But as they begin their journey, something unexpected happens—the rest of the group starts making noise. Loud, unpredictable noise. Some clap their hands, others shout out the person's name, and some even laugh or whistle. The noise is a mix of distractions designed to pull their attention away from the simple task of walking straight through the door.

It's remarkable to watch what happens next. As the noise picks up, the person walking often glances back, sometimes out of curiosity, sometimes in annoyance or confusion. But every time they look back, they lose focus on the path ahead. Their steps become hesitant, and their focus is divided. They try to reorient themselves, but each glance back makes them vulnerable to missteps. More often than not, they walk right into the doorframe, jolting back with a look of frustration or embarrassment.

The lesson here is clear. The moment you start looking back, the path forward becomes clouded. In life, just as in this exercise, distractions will call out to you, tempt you to turn around, to question or doubt your progress. But the goal is to stay focused on what lies ahead, to keep moving forward without being sidetracked by the noise around you. In that moment of walking through the door, the individual experiences firsthand how powerful a single-minded focus can be—and how easy it is to lose that focus when you give in to distraction.

This exercise is a reminder to always keep your eyes on the future, to trust in your own path, and to never look back!

Yes, I've spent a lot of time looking back at the trauma I experienced earlier in my life, way too much time. But over the last eight years, I made the conscious decision to seek out therapy and embark on a healing journey. This process forced me to confront my past and assess how those experiences from so many years ago continue to impact me today—how they shape my decisions in friendships, relationships, and even my professional life. It's been a journey of unraveling the triggers that still provoke the same reactions as they did when I first encountered them.

I recently came across a study that deeply resonated with me. It suggested that trauma is embedded in our DNA and passed down through generations. The study illustrated this with an experiment involving mice. They exposed a mouse to the scent of cherry blossom, which the mouse grew to despise. Remarkably, when that mouse had offspring, the new mice— who had never encountered cherry blossoms—were also traumatized by the scent. This experiment shows how trauma can be inherited even across generations, affecting us in ways we might not even realize.

As a father, this realization has led me to reflect on my own experiences more frequently. I think about the aspects of myself that I need to grow through to be the best example for my daughter. I don't want her to repeat the cycles that have been triggering for me. This awareness has also pushed me to think outside of the box and recognize that what may have been the best approach in the past isn't necessarily the best approach today.

One of the most valuable concepts I've learned through therapy is the idea of "re-parenting" yourself. It's about pausing in those moments of reaction, taking a step back, and reassessing the situation. Sometimes, you have to remind yourself that what you're feeling now isn't necessarily about what's happening in the present. It's about something that happened years ago, something that left a lasting imprint on you.

I've learned to stay in the moment, to differentiate between what's real now and what's a remnant of the past. This practice has transformed how I view my trauma—it's no longer just a burden but a superpower that elevates me in moments of fear and uncertainty. When fear arises, I remind myself of the famous phrase, "It's not going to kill you." I didn't die from those past experiences, and I won't die from facing my fears today. Instead, I'll take the risk, and if I don't succeed, I'll learn.

Reflecting on the past has become a tool for growth, helping me navigate the present and shape a better future for myself and my daughter. It's an ongoing process, but one that empowers me to rise above the trauma and use it as a catalyst for strength and resilience.

THE IMPACT OF TRAUMA AND TRIGGERS

Trauma leaves lasting scars, not just on our bodies but on our hearts and minds. It's as though the past has a tight grip on us, pulling us back into old, familiar pain. Every time we step into a place or face a person tied to our trauma, we risk reopening wounds that never fully healed. These triggers—whether they be a familiar scent, a certain situation, or a particular environment—can flood us with anxiety, despair, or even physical symptoms like headaches and stomachaches.

But the true impact goes deeper. These triggers don't just remind us of the past; they can transport us there, pulling us back into that dark, hopeless place where healing seemed impossible. This emotional chaos can stall our progress, setting us back in the very process that we've worked so hard to move beyond. For those battling addiction, revisiting places tied to past trauma can be especially dangerous—like a cruel reminder of the fragility of recovery. It's clear: healing isn't linear, and it requires vigilance and protection.

MOVE FORWARD, NOT BACKWARD

The act of moving forward is not merely an option—it's a necessity. It's the key to genuine healing, to letting go of the past and stepping into a future where we're no longer controlled by its shadows. When we avoid triggers, we don't just stop reliving pain; we carve out the space necessary for emotional recovery. This space allows us to rebuild ourselves, slowly but surely, with each new moment.

Choosing to move forward also reclaims control over our lives. Trauma often makes us feel powerless; stuck in a cycle we can't break. But when we choose not to return to the places or people that bring back old pain, we reclaim that power. It's a choice of self-respect and self-compassion—one that says, "I am worthy of healing; I am worthy of growth." And this, in turn, reinforces our ability to shape the future we deserve.

Yet, moving forward is easier said than done. But it is possible. Here are some strategies that can help you navigate this journey:

- **Recognize your triggers.** The first step is awareness. Know the people, places, and situations that bring up painful memories. This knowledge helps you protect yourself, making informed choices about where you go and who you spend time with.

- **Set healthy boundaries.** Boundaries are not walls; they are shields to protect your peace. Establish what you need to stay safe and stick to those limits. It's about honoring your journey, not pushing people away, but ensuring that your healing is not compromised.

- **Seek support.** Healing doesn't happen in isolation. Whether it's a therapist or a support group, reaching out for help equips you with the tools to handle your triggers and keep moving forward.

In addition to support, self-care is crucial. Take time for activities that nurture your mind, body, and soul. Whether it's through exercise, meditation, or simply spending time in nature, these practices build resilience and help maintain the strength you need on your journey.

You can also create positive environments that foster healing. Surround yourself with people who uplift and support you, and carve out spaces where you feel safe, nurtured, and free from the risk of re-traumatization.

Healing is a journey. Each step away from the pain of trauma and toward a future of peace and fulfillment is a victory.

THE POWER OF FOCUS

It's easy to be distracted by the noise of the past—the fears, doubts, and regrets. But these distractions are just that: distractions. If we let them pull us away from our path, we risk never reaching our destination. The key is discipline—holding your gaze firmly on the road ahead, no matter how tempting it may be to look back. As Napoleon Hill said, "Self-discipline begins with the mastery of your thoughts. If you don't control what you think, you can't control what you do."

Let me share a powerful story to illustrate this. Satchel Paige, one of the greatest pitchers in baseball history, didn't step onto the Major League field until he was in his forties after years of exclusion due to racism. Yet, despite the years lost, Paige never dwelled on the injustices of the past. Instead, he embraced the opportunities before him, playing with the same mastery that had defined his career in the Negro Leagues. He famously said, "Don't look back. Something might be gaining on you." These words reflect a profound truth: the past can only hold power over us if we let it. When we focus on the future, we move forward with purpose, with strength, and with the wisdom of knowing that the road ahead is where our true power lies.

Let's follow Satchel Paige's wisdom and focus on what's ahead. The past, with all its pain and regret, has no place in the future we're building. Keep moving forward—your future is waiting.

6

TRUST YOUR GUT

"You have to trust your body. Your body will tell you the right thing if you listen to it. It will tell you, 'This is right,' 'This is wrong.'"

—Maya Angelou

A gut feeling is that deep down, knowing you just can't shake it, even if you can't explain it. It's like a voice inside saying, "Trust me on this." Growing up, we might not have been taught to talk about it, but we learned quickly that our instincts can save us. A gut feeling isn't based on logic or some plan you wrote down—it's what you feel in your body like a warning light or a quiet sense of calm telling you what's up. It's that sense you get about a person or situation before your mind even has the words for it. When you come from a place where survival means reading between the lines, you know your gut is usually right. Trusting it is about knowing you've got your own back, even if no one else does.

There have been times in my life when I didn't trust my gut, and I've often regretted it. For example, I knew deep down it was time to leave the corporate world, but I ignored that gut feeling, convincing myself to stick it out a little longer. I kept asking myself, "Could I really make it on my own?" The security of a steady paycheck and benefits was hard to walk away from, even though every fiber in me felt like I was out of place, just going through the motions. I'd gotten so used to the routine and the title that I second-guessed whether I could succeed without it.

My gut told me I was meant for something different, something that allowed me to build, to create, and to feel free, but I kept trying to quiet that voice. The fear of failure kept me stuck, wondering if I had what it took to make way for myself. Looking back, not listening to my gut cost me time and peace, but it taught me that there comes a point where staying safe feels riskier than stepping into the unknown.

It goes all the way back to my days in Detroit. Growing up in a single-parent home, I witnessed the struggles and heartache that came with broken relationships. The last thing I wanted was to repeat those patterns in my own life. But the fear of ending up like my parents sometimes clouded my judgment, leading me to second-guess myself when I should have trusted my instincts.

There were moments when my gut told me that someone was good for me, but I didn't listen. I let doubts and insecurities creep in, convincing myself that they were trying to trick me or that they would eventually leave. These thoughts often led me to overreact, pushing people away who might have been great partners or friends. I'd find myself having to go back to them, admitting that I overreacted, and realizing that we could have had something special—something that was lost because I didn't trust myself.

Today, I've learned to approach relationships, both romantic and platonic, with a different mindset. I've become more forward-thinking and more attuned to looking into someone's heart and seeing if I can find a reflection of myself in them. I ask myself if we share the same values and if our visions for one another align. These are the questions that now guide my thinking, helping me to make better decisions without being held back by a lack of trust in myself.

I've also come to understand that making a good decision doesn't always mean choosing something that benefits me in the immediate sense. Sometimes, saying no is the best decision I can make, even if it's difficult. Rejecting what isn't a good fit for me is just as important as embracing what is. It's taken time, but I've learned that trusting my gut isn't just about making the right choices—it's about trusting myself to handle whatever outcome those choices bring.

Looking back, I see how not trusting my gut has shaped my journey, especially in relationships. But I also see how I've grown from those experiences. I've learned to trust myself more to be okay with the decisions I make, even if they don't always lead to the outcome I expected. While I can't change the past, I can take those lessons forward, ensuring that today, I trust my gut and make choices that align with who I am and who I want to be.

WHAT IS YOUR GUT?

Have you ever felt something in the pit of your stomach— a sense of rightness—yet couldn't quite explain why? That's your gut speaking to you. Your intuition is a powerful internal compass, subtly guiding you through life's complexities and uncertainties. Trusting your gut doesn't just help you make decisions; it transforms your life, leading you toward a deeper sense of fulfillment. But in a world that often prioritizes logic and data over feelings, how do we reconnect with and trust that inner voice?

Intuition is the quiet whisper within, the inexplicable feeling or hunch that emerges when you're at a crossroads. It's knowing what to do without understanding why, a blend of past experiences, instincts, and subconscious knowledge. Intuition operates beneath the surface, processing information your conscious mind doesn't fully grasp. It's that subtle nudge that tells you to take an unexpected route or seize an opportunity that feels too right to ignore. Though it may seem mysterious, intuition is one of the most powerful tools you possess.

Trusting your gut can save you from pitfalls that logic alone might miss. Logic is based on data, patterns, and facts—but it's often too rigid to capture the full picture. Intuition offers a broader perspective, alerting you to unseen dangers or possibilities that data doesn't account for. It's the red flag that appears when a decision doesn't feel aligned or the spark of inspiration that leads you down a path you hadn't considered. Trusting your intuition adds depth to your decision-making, empowering you to navigate the unknown with more confidence.

When you learn to trust your gut, you elevate your decision-making abilities. Your intuition gives you a holistic view, considering emotions, body sensations, and subtle cues that logic overlooks. For example, in a business situation, your gut might sense underlying tensions in a partnership that data doesn't show. Listening to that intuitive insight allows you to make strategic, well-rounded choices.

Moreover, trusting your intuition strengthens your self-trust. Each time you follow your gut and see positive outcomes, your confidence grows. This internal validation creates a cycle: the more you trust yourself, the more attuned you become to your inner wisdom, and the more capable you feel in navigating life's challenges.

Intuition also fuels creativity. When you listen to that quiet inner voice, you unlock new ideas and possibilities that may not fit within conventional frameworks. Your gut can push you beyond the limits of logic, encouraging you to take risks, explore uncharted territory, and find solutions that set you apart. In this way, intuition isn't just a decision-making tool—it's a gateway to innovation and personal growth.

HOW TO INTERPRET YOUR GUT

So, how can you tune into this powerful guide? Start by paying attention to your body. Your body speaks a language that your conscious mind may not fully understand, but it holds the answers. Does your stomach tighten when faced with a difficult choice? Does your chest feel light and expansive when you're on the right path? These physical sensations are the early warnings and affirmations of your intuition.

Listening to your inner voice is another key practice. Your intuition doesn't shout—it whispers. It's the quiet voice beneath the noise of daily life, offering gentle guidance that cuts through confusion. Learn to differentiate between the constant chatter of your thoughts and the quiet nudges of your gut. The more you listen, the clearer that voice becomes.

Mindfulness is an excellent tool for strengthening your connection to intuition. When you practice mindfulness, you ground yourself in the present moment, becoming more aware of your feelings, thoughts, and physical sensations. This awareness enhances your ability to recognize intuitive signals. Meditation, deep breathing, and other mindfulness practices can cultivate this connection.

To build trust in your gut, start small. Make everyday decisions based on your intuition and observe the outcomes. Over time, you'll see patterns emerge, helping you refine your ability to discern your gut's true messages. Remember, it's normal to feel doubt or hesitation—especially if you've been conditioned to rely on logic. But trusting your intuition is a practice, and with every step, your confidence in this powerful tool will grow.

It's important to remember that intuition and logic are not opposites; they complement each other. Use your gut to guide you, and then validate your insights with logic. This balanced approach allows you to make decisions that honor both your instincts and the facts.

Another useful strategy is journaling your intuitive experiences. Document moments when you trusted your gut and reflect on the results. Keep track of how you felt at the time and how the situation unfolded. Over time, you'll begin to see patterns and gain greater clarity about how your intuition communicates with you. This practice builds trust and strengthens your connection to your inner wisdom.

Above all, be patient with yourself. Trusting your intuition is a skill that takes time to develop. You may not always get it right, but every step you take toward trusting your gut is a step toward a more empowered, authentic life.

There was a time when I always knew, deep down, that I was meant to help kids through robotics. I could picture it: teaching them the skills that would open doors, help them build confidence, and spark a sense of possibility they might not have found elsewhere. But I pushed it aside. I wasn't ready, I told myself. I needed more experience, more stability, more time. That persistent pull—the one that reminded me how robotics had changed my own life—was too easy to ignore.

For years, I convinced myself it was just a dream, something I would do "one day." But eventually, that feeling became undeniable. It wasn't just a gut feeling; it was my soul speaking. So, I finally took the leap, and today, I've had the privilege of helping thousands of kids see a future in robotics. Now, looking back, I realize that following my purpose was the only choice that truly made sense.

Take a moment now. Close your eyes and listen to your gut. Are you truly honoring that inner voice, that instinct that knows where you need to go—even when logic or fear might pull you in another direction? Life moves fast, and it's easy to ignore that voice amidst the chaos. But in the stillness, your gut is often the clearest guide. Reflect on whether you're honoring that intuition or pushing it aside. Allow yourself the space to reconnect with what feels right, and let it lead you forward with purpose.

7

TAKE THAT RISK

"If there is no struggle, there is no progress."

—Fredrick Douglas

When I first stepped into the role of mentoring young people, I knew it was a risk. It wasn't just the time and energy I was investing. It was the vulnerability required to connect with kids who had every reason not to trust me. As an engineer mentoring a group of high school students in robotics, I quickly realized that gaining their trust wasn't going to be easy.

From the start, they questioned whether I was truly one of them. My mentor, Ray, introduced me to the group with, "Who wants to meet a black robot engineer?" The kids looked at me with skepticism as if to say, "Are you really from Detroit or just claiming it?" They couldn't reconcile the person standing before them—well-dressed, successful—with the gritty image they had of their city. To them, I was too polished, too different. It was clear that if I wanted to make a real impact, I would have to break through their doubts and show them who I really was by peeling back a few layers.

Among the students was a young man who connected with me more than the others, though the trust wasn't immediate.

His name was Delon. Delon wanted to go into computer programming, and I was his mentor during his time on the robotics team. He was passionate about computer programming and became the lead programmer on his high school's robotics team. I was his mentor during that time, helping to guide him through the challenges and responsibilities of being part of such a technical, high-stakes environment. Delon had a natural talent for coding, and it was clear he was committed to learning and growing in this field. But our connection went beyond just robotics.

In many ways, Delon's background mirrored mine. Like me, he grew up in a single-parent household, living with his mother, sister, and grandmother. That was my family dynamic, too—a house full of strong women where, as the only boy, there was a sense of responsibility that came early. I understood Delon in a way that went beyond just being his mentor on the robotics team. I knew what it was like to feel that unspoken pressure to take care of your family, to be the one who holds everything together.

As we worked together, our bond deepened. It was fulfilling to see him thrive in programming and robotics, but when it came time for him to make the leap to college, that's when things got tough. Delon had been accepted to Tennessee State, which was a great opportunity for him to continue his education and grow as a programmer. But he struggled with the idea of leaving home. That same sense of responsibility I had felt growing up was now weighing heavily on him. He didn't want to leave his mother, sister, and grandmother behind. He felt like it was his job to take care of them.

I did my best to help him see the bigger picture—that going to college could ultimately help him take even better care of his family in the long run. But despite all the conversations we had, the encouragement, and the plans we made for him to go to Tennessee State, it didn't happen. The pull of home was too strong, and Delon ended up coming back. It was a difficult moment, not just for him but for me as well. I understood his decision on a personal level, but I also knew how much potential he had and how hard it could be to make the choice to step out into the unknown.

One day, I called to check in on him. He told me his car had broken down and that he had expanded his attention to desperate measures to make some money. At that moment, I was faced with a choice: keep our conversation light and casual or take the risk of telling him the truth about my past. Initially, I chose the safer route, speaking to him in drug terms trying to relate on a surface level. But later, I couldn't shake the feeling that I had failed him by not being honest.

The next day, I took the risk. I called him back and told him the full story of my own experiences—how I had sold drugs, how I had lost friends to violence, and how dangerous that path truly was. It was a gamble. I knew he looked up to me, and revealing my past could either strengthen our bond or shatter the image he had of me. But I couldn't let him continue down the road he was on without knowing the truth.

I didn't stop there. I had just bought a new home, and though I wasn't planning on replacing my car so soon, I saw an opportunity. I purchased a new truck, and I gave him my old car so he could get to his certification classes, making it clear that selling drugs was not an option. I took a leap of faith, hoping that this gesture and my honesty would push him toward a better future.

The risk paid off. He used that car to finish his certification, landed a job in IT support, and began turning his life around. He even started a skateboard business and talked about running for mayor of Detroit. Years later, when I saw him again, he ran up to me on the Detroit riverfront and gave me a hug. It was a powerful moment that affirmed the risk I took was worth it.

By opening up and sharing the darker parts of my life, I was able to connect with him in a way that changed the course of his future. Mentorship isn't just about teaching skills; it's about taking risks, being vulnerable, and trusting that your honesty will resonate with those who need it most. That risk I took—revealing my past, giving him my car, and believing in his potential—paid off in ways I could never have imagined. He wasn't just another student; he became a success story, one that continues to remind me why taking risks in mentorship is always worth it.

WHY TAKE RISKS?

Life is a series of choices, each carrying its own risks and rewards. Society often nudges us toward playing it safe, sticking with what's familiar and predictable. Yet, what if playing it safe is the riskiest move of all? Staying in our comfort zones can lead to a life of stagnation—one where we miss out on growth, innovation, and fulfillment

Taking risks, particularly calculated ones, is the gateway to transformation. It's where we stretch ourselves beyond our limits, discover our potential, and uncover opportunities that would otherwise remain hidden.

THE NECESSITY OF RISK

Why is taking risks so essential? On the surface, staying in your comfort zone feels secure, but comfort is often a slow road to dissatisfaction. Growth doesn't thrive in the realm of the predictable. It requires stepping into the unknown, confronting fears, and embracing the challenge of uncertainty.

Taking risks pushes us to uncover strengths and navigate weaknesses. It's an arena where personal growth flourishes. Each risk you embrace teaches you resilience, builds character, and helps you uncover new dimensions of yourself.

THE OPPORTUNITY IN RISK

Think about the world's most impactful entrepreneurs, artists, and leaders. What if they had chosen safety over audacity? Without risk, innovation, creativity, and progress would stall. Risks are the bridges to new possibilities—unexpected connections, transformative experiences, and milestones on the path to achieving your goals.

Moreover, risk-taking builds confidence. Every time you step out of your comfort zone and achieve even modest success, your self-belief strengthens. Even when outcomes aren't as expected, the act of trying builds resilience. This cumulative confidence makes it easier to tackle future challenges with courage and tenacity.

CREATIVITY AND RISK

Risk-taking also fuels creativity and innovation. The unknown forces you to think differently, innovate, and solve problems in novel ways. In environments that embrace risk, failure isn't the enemy—it's a stepping stone to breakthroughs.

CALCULATED RISKS: THE KEY TO SUCCESS

Risk doesn't mean recklessness. It's about calculation and purpose. Before taking a leap, weigh the benefits against potential downsides. Ask yourself: What's the best possible outcome? The worst? How will I navigate either scenario? This deliberate approach ensures risks align with your goals and values, giving you the clarity to proceed boldly.

EMBRACING UNCERTAINTY

Uncertainty is an inseparable part of risk. While intimidating, it's also where growth and discovery happen. Each step into the unknown is a chance to learn, evolve, and achieve things you once thought impossible.

OVERCOMING THE FEAR OF FAILURE

Fear and risk go hand-in-hand. Fear of failure is a natural reaction—but it's also a hurdle you can overcome. Writing this book, for instance, was a risk for me—a choice shadowed by doubts and fears of inadequacy. Yet, here I am, embracing it.

How can you conquer your fear of failure?

1. **Reframe Failure**: Shift your perspective. Failure isn't an endpoint; it's an invaluable teacher. Every misstep is a lesson, moving you closer to success.

2. **Focus on Rewards**: Instead of fixating on what could go wrong, envision what could go right. Positive visualization helps you channel energy toward your goals.

3. **Practice Mindfulness**: Techniques like meditation and deep breathing ground you in the present, easing anxiety about the unknown.

4. **Act Despite Fear**: Courage isn't the absence of fear; it's moving forward in its presence. The more you practice this, the more fearless you'll become.

THE TRANSFORMATIVE POWER OF RISK

Taking risks can reshape your life in ways you've never imagined. Start small if you must—take manageable steps outside your comfort zone. Over time, as your confidence grows, so will your willingness to embrace bigger challenges.

Remember, the greatest risks often carry the greatest rewards. Surround yourself with people who encourage you, learn from both success and failure and remain open to life's possibilities. In doing so, you'll find that risk isn't a gamble—it's a necessary ingredient for growth, fulfillment, and transformation.

Embrace the power of risk, and let it illuminate paths you never knew existed.

8

THE ART OF OPTIONS

"Never limit yourself because of others' limited imagination; never limit others because of your own limited imagination."

—Mae Jamison

My upbringing in Detroit provided me with a particular view of the world shaped by the streets, the people, and the grit that comes from growing up in a city with its own kind of heartbeat. My experiences weren't like most people were there at the time, and they taught me to stay tough, stay focused, and know when to push forward. So, in 2004, when I became the Lead Robotics Engineer for the Hummer H3 project, I stepped into a world I'd only ever seen from a distance. It was somewhat of a shock to me.

First off, I noticed that Confederate flags were every-where—on hats, cars, shirts, and even stickers around the plant. For someone like me, a black man from Detroit, this could have been unsettling, even intimidating, like a silent message that I was an outsider in more ways than one. I was in the South now, in a place with its own history and symbols that carried heavy meanings. These flags weren't just deco-rations; they were reminders of a past that, for many, like me, still felt painfully close to the surface. It was as if the environment itself was saying, "You don't belong here." But I had made it this far, and I wasn't about to let symbols—or the weight of history—push me out. I reminded myself why I was there and leaned on the resilience that had brought me through countless challenges before.

So, I didn't let it shake me. I'd learned long ago to read a room, and this time, I chose not to react, to keep my focus steady. I wasn't there to change anyone's mind, and I didn't need their validation. I was there to do what I knew best: lead, innovate, and succeed. Instead of letting fear or anger take over, I zeroed in on the job at hand, knowing that every step I took, every goal I hit, was proof that I belonged right where I was. It wasn't just about proving myself to others—it was about proving to myself that I could navigate any space, no matter what symbols were hanging on the walls.

There was a lesson in patience and understanding the value of choosing how to react. During that time, a black preacher who worked as a safety foreman would check in on me every day. He would remind me that I was the only black person doing anything of significance on that plant, which was true. While others were on the assembly line, I was programming robots. But instead of feeling isolated or reacting emotionally, I appreciated the support he and others provided. He assured me that if I ever needed anything, I had people praying for me. His kindness reminded me that sometimes, the best option is to acknowledge support where it's offered and not let surface-level differences dictate my experience.

Though the Confederate flags were a constant presence, none of the men in the plant ever crossed the line. Sure, they asked where I was from or called me a "Yankee," but it was more curiosity than hostility. Instead of jumping to conclusions, I recognized that they might not have seen many people like me programming robots. There was an undercurrent of envy or surprise, but I didn't let that distract me. It was a matter of staying calm, assessing the situation, and deciding how to respond without making rash judgments.

Six months into my role as the lead robotics engineer overseeing the Hummer H3 project, I encountered my first dilemma as a leader. We had just under two weeks during the Christmas break to program over 100 robots and ensure that everything was back online without a hitch. The deadline was tight, and I knew we needed a flawless launch after the break. Instead of panicking, I prepared carefully, hiring a team of ten programmers to help.

One of the programmers, however, turned out to be unreliable. He had a habit of drinking after work and showing up late, and when it came to programming, he just couldn't seem to follow my instructions. The first time he deleted an entire robot program, I calmly restored the backup I had prepared, knowing that preparation gave me options in case something went wrong. When he made the same mistake again, I didn't react impulsively or let frustration take over. Instead, I considered my options and realized he was setting us back. I needed a solution that would help the team succeed.

I consulted with my senior robot programmer, taking time to weigh my options rather than making a hasty decision. We both agreed that letting him go was the best course of action. It wasn't an easy choice, especially right before Christmas, but I didn't let the emotional weight of the decision cloud my judgment. By letting him go, I was giving myself—and the rest of the team—a better chance of meeting the deadline without unnecessary setbacks.

After letting him go, I took on more work myself and redistributed tasks among the remaining team members. I didn't react out of frustration; I adjusted, knowing that the key to success was in managing resources carefully and avoiding impulsive decisions. We worked longer hours, but because I had calmly assessed the situation and made thoughtful decisions, we successfully launched the robots on time after the break.

This experience taught me a valuable lesson in leadership: giving yourself options and thinking through your responses are crucial, especially when managing a team. If I had let frustration guide me, I might have made rash decisions that derailed the entire project. Instead, by staying calm, considering all my options, and planning for potential setbacks, I was able to lead the team to success. The key was in not reacting impulsively but allowing myself the space to make informed, calculated choices, which ultimately led to achieving the project's goals.

THE DANGER OF KNEE-JERK REACTIONS

Life often throws us into situations where we must make quick decisions. The urge to react instantly, driven by emotion, is strong. However, knee-jerk reactions can lead to regrettable consequences. The art of giving yourself options lies in resisting the impulse to react hastily and instead taking the time to explore different possibilities. This approach not only helps us make better decisions but also ensures that we remain in control of our choices and their outcomes.

Knee-jerk reactions are often based on immediate emotions rather than careful consideration. When faced with a challenging situation, our initial response might be driven by fear, anger, or frustration. This limited perspective can cloud our judgment and lead to impulsive decisions that we might later regret.

For example, reacting out of anger during a disagreement can result in harsh words that damage relationships. Similarly, making a financial decision in a moment of panic can lead to poor investments or missed opportunities. Knee-jerk reactions often close off avenues that might have been more beneficial if given proper consideration.

The regret that follows a hasty decision can be a heavy burden. Realizing that a different approach might have led to a better outcome can be painful. This regret is a stark reminder of the importance of taking the time to explore our options before making decisions.

THE POWER OF OPTIONS

Giving yourself options broadens your perspective and allows you to consider different possibilities and outcomes. This approach helps in making decisions based on logic and sound reasoning rather than immediate emotions. When you take the time to weigh various options, you can foresee potential challenges and benefits, leading to more informed and balanced decisions.

For instance, when faced with a career choice, considering different job opportunities and their long-term impact can lead to a more satisfying career path. In personal relationships, thinking through the possible repercussions of your actions can help maintain harmony and understanding.

By giving yourself options, you also create a buffer against stress. Knowing that you have considered various scenarios and are prepared for different outcomes can reduce anxiety and increase your confidence in your decision-making abilities. This practice builds resilience and equips you to handle future challenges more effectively.

HOW TO GIVE YOURSELF OPTIONS

To cultivate the habit of giving yourself options, start by slowing down. When confronted with a decision, take a step back and breathe. This pause allows you to calm your emotions and approach the situation with a clearer mind. Remind yourself that it's okay to take time before responding.

Consider all possibilities, even those that seem unlikely or unfavorable. This comprehensive evaluation ensures that you don't overlook any potential solutions. List out the pros and cons of each option to help visualize the potential outcomes. This exercise can provide clarity and highlight the best course of action.

Consult with others to gain different perspectives. Sometimes, an outside opinion can shed light on aspects you hadn't considered. Trusted friends, family members, or colleagues can offer valuable insights and help you see the situation from different angles.

Using a pro/con list can be particularly effective. Writing down the advantages and disadvantages of each option can help you objectively assess your choices. This tangible method makes the decision-making process more structured and less overwhelming. Overcoming the impulse to react impulsively requires practice and self-awareness. Start by recognizing your emotional triggers. Understanding what provokes a knee-jerk reaction can help you anticipate and manage these responses.

Another effective strategy is to create a mental checklist for decision-making. When faced with a choice, run through this checklist to ensure you've considered all options and consulted the necessary resources. This habit can become second nature over time, helping you make more deliberate decisions.

Cultivating patience is also crucial. Trust that taking the time to consider your options will lead to better outcomes. Remind yourself that immediate reactions are rarely the best course of action. Developing patience allows you to approach decisions with a calm and collected mindset.

STAYING CENTERED IN CHALLENGING ENVIRONMENTS

Finally, if you find yourself in an environment that is particularly hostile or toxic, stay anchored in your faith and inner self. Refuse to let your surroundings dictate who you are or how you feel. Hostile environments can try to shape you, wearing down your confidence and testing your patience, but your power lies in choosing how you respond.

Stay centered on your values, and give yourself emotional options by stepping back, assessing what's really important, and remembering why you're there. Protect your peace by setting internal boundaries—decide what you're willing to engage with and what you'll let slide.

Cultivating this kind of emotional flexibility allows you to focus on your goals without absorbing negativity from the environment around you. Ultimately, it's about holding on to your sense of purpose and refusing to give that power away, no matter how challenging the circumstances. Whatever you do, don't allow yourself to be put into a corner where you have no options!

9

CAKE: HAVE IT, OR EAT IT!

"Not everything that is faced can be changed,
but nothing can be changed until it is faced."

—James Baldwin

After I graduated from high school, my life lacked direction and my purpose was fading as I still found myself running the streets. In August 1996, my favorite rap group, UGK released the album Ridin' Dirty. As I rode down the street listening from start to finish, I began to feel like the songs were about my life. As I sang, "One day you're here, baby. And then you're gone…" I realized I wasn't living; I was surviving. It felt like a rite of passage, but it was also a trap. I drove from one block to the next, filling time with moments that seemed like they mattered—until they didn't. I had run-ins with the police, came too close to trouble too many times, and attended more funerals than I could count. Friends, foes, and faces that blurred together in a haze of grief and anger. Each goodbye felt like a warning, yet I couldn't seem to pull myself out.

Disgusted with what I saw around me and the choices I was making, I searched for a way out. My escape came in the form of a chance to attend Alabama State University. The first year was a whirlwind, but by the end of it, I found myself at a crossroads. For the first time, I stood in a quiet moment and truly understood the weight of my choices. There was the comfort of the life I knew—familiar, predictable, and dark—and then there was this new path, one that felt like it was meant for me but was just out of reach. I knew that I was calling myself toward something bigger, something purposeful. I realized I had to choose between drifting in the direction I'd always gone or daring to step toward the unknown. That moment marked the beginning of my journey to redefine who I was and what I could become.

I often think about a story from that time, one that involved Mr. Johnson, who was like the father of our block back in Detroit. Mr. Johnson was a tough, loving man who made sure everyone stayed on track and protected the neighborhood in ways that most people don't bother to do anymore.

I remember coming home from college one summer, eager to reconnect with old friends. Mrs. Jennings, a dear neighbor, picked me up and dropped me off at home. I told her I'd stop by her house after I settled in, but as I was walking down the street, I saw Mr. Johnson sitting on his porch. He called out to me, "Hey, Smoke, where are you going?"

"I'm heading down to the corner to see my friends," I replied.

But Mr. Johnson wasn't having it. He said, "No, you're not. Come here." He explained that my friends had been hanging out on that same corner ever since I left for college and hadn't done anything with their lives. He was adamant that I couldn't go back to that corner, telling me, "You're in college now. You've got a new life. You can't have this old life and your new life at the same time."

At first, I laughed it off. "Come on, Mr. Johnson, you're tripping."

But he was serious. He looked me dead in the eye and said, "That can't be your life anymore. You've got to leave that behind. It's over. They're not going where you're going."

I tried to argue, saying these were the only friends I'd known my whole life, but he wouldn't budge. He told me he'd give me five minutes with my friends, and if I wasn't back, he'd come down there with his shotgun. And trust me, he was known for doing just that my entire childhood. He was the one who restored order whenever things got too rowdy in the neighborhood, and we all respected him for it.

So, I went to see my friends. We laughed and caught up on my college experience, but I deliberately took my time, curious to see if Mr. Johnson would follow through. Sure enough, he came down with his shotgun, put his arm around me, and told my friends, "Smoke isn't hanging out with you guys anymore. He's in college now, going to a different place." He pointed out that while they had spent the whole year on that same corner, I was moving on.

It was then I realized I had to make a choice. After leaving the corner, I went to see Mrs. Jennings and her husband. They echoed Mr. Johnson's words, saying my friends hadn't made any decisions about their lives yet. As much as I loved them, it was clear I couldn't have it both ways—I couldn't hold on to the life I knew while pursuing the one I was meant for.

That summer, I spent a lot of time thinking about my future. I ended up getting a job at Ford Motor Company, working the second shift. It was the summer of 1998, and I had just finished my first year at Alabama State University. I took the job because I needed the money, but it was tough. Working on the assembly line was grueling, especially when they put me in the pit, where cars passed overhead, and I had to fasten five bolts into place with a heavy torque tool. My body ached in ways I had never experienced before. The money was good, but the work was physically demanding, and I knew this wasn't where my dreams lay.

About two weeks before I was set to return to school, my shift supervisor asked if I wanted to stay and keep working or go back to college. I could have stayed and made enough time to get into the union, but after some thought, I realized that while the job provided stability, it wasn't my calling. I didn't see myself working on the line forever. So, I made the choice to return to school and started my first year at Tennessee State University.

That summer taught me an important lesson: you can't have it both ways. I had to choose between making quick money or pursuing a long-term career as an engineer. While it was tempting to stay in the comfort of what I knew, I'm glad I chose the path that aligned with my goals and dreams.

THE FALLACY OF HAVING IT BOTH WAYS

Life has a peculiar way of testing us with choices that seem impossible to reconcile. We dream of having it all—success and serenity, indulgence and security, love and independence—but reality often has other plans. Resources are finite, and conflicting priorities demand that we choose. Yet, the allure of trying to "have it both ways" is strong, even when it sets us up for frustration and failure.

Think about it: you can't spend hours at work chasing the next promotion and expect to nurture deep personal connections at the same time. Nor can you splurge on luxury vacations while building a rock-solid financial future without compromise. These trade-offs are a reality we all face. Attempting to dodge them only leads to stress and outcomes that fall short of our aspirations.

The first step to making better decisions is embracing this truth—acknowledging that life is full of competing priorities. The key lies not in avoiding hard choices but in making them wisely, with clarity and purpose.

THE COST OF SPLITTING FOCUS

Life constantly forces us to prioritize, whether it's between professional ambitions and family, personal growth and social obligations, or health and convenience. Trying to give equal weight to every area often leads to mediocrity across the board. You become the proverbial jack of all trades, master of none.

Imagine a tightrope walker carrying two heavy bags, trying to balance while inching forward. The heavier the load on both sides, the harder it becomes to move without faltering. Now, imagine choosing one bag that is lighter, purposeful, and aligned with your goals. The path forward becomes steadier and more achievable.

Prioritizing means letting go of the idea that everything can be done perfectly at once. It's about choosing what matters most and being at peace with what must wait.

THE GROWTH IN TOUGH CHOICES

There's a transformative power in making tough decisions. Each choice we make stretches us beyond our comfort zones, illuminating our values, strengths, and limitations. These moments of clarity build resilience, teaching us not only to endure challenges but to thrive in their wake.

Consider the young professional who sacrifices late-night parties to pursue an advanced degree. The hours spent studying may feel grueling, but the payoff—a fulfilling career, financial security, and personal growth—far outweighs the temporary discomfort. Tough choices demand courage, but they also yield profound rewards.

HOW TO MAKE DECISIONS THAT MATTER

To master the art of decision-making, start with self-awareness. What are your core values? What goals truly matter to you? By identifying your priorities, you can filter out distractions and focus your energy where it counts.

Once your priorities are clear, evaluate your options thoughtfully. Create a list of pros and cons, weighing each against your values and long-term goals. Visualizing potential outcomes can bring structure to what might otherwise feel like an overwhelming process.

Be prepared to compromise. Every gain comes with a cost, whether it's time, money, or comfort. Success often requires sacrifices, but those sacrifices are worthwhile when they align with your greater purpose.

Finally, trust yourself. Every decision you make, even the imperfect ones, is a step forward. Confidence in your ability to decide—and learn from outcomes—will help you navigate life's complexities with grace.

A VISION FOR THE FUTURE

As Kobe Bryant once said, "When you make a choice and say, 'Come hell or high water, I am going to be this,' then you should not be surprised when you are that." His words remind us that our decisions shape our destiny. When we commit to a path wholeheartedly, the results often feel like destiny fulfilled.

So, what choice will you make today? Will you continue trying to have it both ways or will you embrace the clarity that comes from prioritizing what truly matters? Life's tough decisions are not obstacles; they are opportunities to grow, achieve, and live with purpose.

By making deliberate choices, sacrificing where necessary, and trusting in your ability to adapt, you can craft a life that feels not just successful but deeply fulfilling. Remember, the art of decision-making improves with practice, and each step you take builds the life you envision.

10

LIFE ISN'T A LAB

"Life is about not knowing, having to change, taking the moment and making the best of it, without knowing what's going to happen next."

—Gilda Radner

For much of my life, I've wrestled with the need for perfection. As a Black man, I've often felt I don't have the luxury of making mistakes. Excellence is the standard from which I come, but extraordinary has always been my goal.

As an engineer, the drive for perfection feels almost second nature. It's a mindset ingrained through years of training: a constant push to produce work that is flawless, to ensure every detail is accounted for, and every potential issue is preemptively addressed. On the surface, this pursuit seems noble. Precision and thoroughness are vital when working with complex systems where even minor errors can lead to significant consequences. Perfectionism, in this sense, has its merits.

Being a perfectionist offers certain advantages. When you've checked every nook and cranny, dotted every "i," and crossed every "t," you can deliver with confidence. It's a reassuring feeling—the certainty that your work will stand up to scrutiny. People look at the finished product and think, "He's thought of everything." That's the kind of impression I've always strived to leave.

But perfectionism has a dark side, one that has cost me more than I'd like to admit. Time and time again, I've found myself overcomplicating tasks that should have been simple. A straightforward request transforms into a monumental project as I try to account for every conceivable scenario. Deadlines slip by, opportunities vanish, and I'm left holding a piece of work that, while polished, never saw the light of day because I took too long to release it.

The hardest lesson for me to learn has been this: sometimes, "good enough" really is good enough. Not every situation demands exhaustive detail or painstaking refinement. There's a balance to be struck between striving for excellence and knowing when to let go. I've had to confront my fear that anything less than perfection would reflect poorly on me. In doing so, I've discovered that many of the fears I held were unfounded.

The truth is chasing perfection can become a trap, an endless cycle of doubt and delay. It can hold you back from taking risks and embracing opportunities that require you to act now rather than later. Trusting yourself means accepting that imperfections are not failures—they're steps on the journey.

Moving forward without constantly looking back has taught me the value of progress over perfection. It's not about lowering my standards; it's about expanding my understanding of success. Sometimes, success is about delivering with heart and intention, even if the execution isn't flawless. Sometimes, it's about letting your work speak for itself, imperfections and all.

Take writing about myself, for instance. I detest it. I'd much rather speak about my experiences than write them down. There's something about the permanence of words on paper that makes me overthink every phrase, every sentence. But I've learned that it's okay to let someone else do the writing while I do the talking. Even if the end product doesn't perfectly reflect how I would have written it, I've come to realize that others often love it, sometimes even more than I would.

This mindset shift—accepting that nothing is ever truly perfect—has been liberating. As an engineer, you know that there's always something that can be improved. The pursuit of perfection is endless, and if you're not careful, it can paralyze you. But when you recognize that good enough is often all you need, you free yourself to make progress, take risks, and iterate on your work. There's always another version, another chance to refine and perfect in the future.

This reminds me of one of my favorite examples: Steve Jobs and the iPhone. When the iPhone was first released, it was a masterpiece. It worked seamlessly, without bugs, because Jobs was a perfectionist. He refused to release the software until it was exactly right. But this meticulous approach had its downsides. The pace of innovation was slower than stakeholders liked, and eventually, that led to Jobs being replaced by Tim Cook, whose approach was more in line with the typical business mindset: just release it and fix the bugs later.

Under Cook, the iPhone evolved rapidly, and profits soared as Apple beat the competition to the market time and again. But for those who were loyal to the brand, the experience wasn't quite the same. Frequent updates and persistent bugs became the norm, and the frustration of constantly having to update the phone every other week was palpable. The trade-off was clear: greater speed and profitability, but at the cost of the flawless experience that had once defined the product.

The lesson here is clear: perfection has its place, but so does pragmatism. There's a balance to be struck between striving for perfection and knowing when it's time to release your work into the world. This is a lesson I'm learning to embrace more fully every day. In the past, my perfectionism might have held me back, but now I understand the importance of simply getting started.

THE PERFECTION TRAP

In a world that glorifies flawlessness, it's easy to fall into the illusion that life should be lived without mistakes, missteps, or unpredictability. But let me share a truth that can set you free: life is not a perfectly calibrated experiment, nor should it be. Life is gloriously messy, rich with unexpected turns, and alive with variation. Embracing this variation, rather than chasing perfection, isn't just necessary—it's transformative.

The pursuit of perfection is a slippery slope. It sets us on a course toward unreachable ideals, laden with anxiety, self-doubt, and eventual burnout. The harder we chase the illusion of perfection, the more elusive it becomes. It's like chasing a mirage in the desert—always just out of reach. This relentless quest doesn't only exhaust us; it stifles our creativity and growth, trapping us in a narrow, joyless loop of self-criticism.

At its heart, perfectionism is a fear of failure. It convinces us that mistakes are fatal and risks are too dangerous to take. But this fear doesn't protect us—it paralyzes us. It keeps us locked in our comfort zones, where the potential is stifled, experiences are limited, and life becomes a shadow of what it could be.

Even worse, perfectionism fosters a harsh inner critic. It magnifies our flaws while diminishing our successes, eroding our self-esteem one critique at a time. The joy of simply being—of existing as you are—is replaced by a never-ending dissatisfaction with what you are not.

REFRAMING THE NARRATIVE: EMBRACING VARIATION

Here's a liberating idea: perfection is an illusion, but variation is reality. The word "imperfection" carries a negative charge that doesn't serve us, so let's discard it. Instead, let's call it what it really is: **variation**.

Variation isn't a flaw—it's the essence of life itself. Embracing it means recognizing that life's beauty lies in its diversity, unpredictability, and dynamic nature. By accepting this truth, we release ourselves from the rigid grip of perfectionism and open our arms to the richness of the human experience.

When we embrace variation, we celebrate differences. Each of us is a masterpiece of unique strengths, weaknesses, and experiences. These differences don't diminish us—they enhance us. They make our communities vibrant and our relationships profound.

Embracing variation also cultivates resilience. Life is unpredictable, and plans rarely unfold as intended. By becoming comfortable with variation, we learn to adapt, pivot, and thrive in the face of change. This resilience fuels personal growth, fortifies our spirit, and prepares us to navigate life's inevitable challenges.

Even more, variation fosters authenticity. When we stop trying to conform to an impossible ideal and instead accept ourselves as we are, we connect more deeply with others. Authenticity builds trust, intimacy, and genuine relationships. It's through our real, unpolished selves that we find true fulfillment.

And then there's creativity. Every creative mind understands that variation is not the enemy—it's the spark. Mistakes become opportunities, and out-of-the-box thinking flourishes when we embrace the unexpected. Creativity thrives not in the pursuit of perfection but in the freedom to explore, to fail, and to try again.

PRACTICAL STEPS TO EMBRACE VARIATION

1. **Start with self-acceptance.**

   Reflect on your strengths and acknowledge your weaknesses—not with judgment, but with understanding. Perfection isn't the goal; self-awareness and self-compassion are.

2. **Celebrate diversity.**

   Seek out people with different backgrounds, perspectives, and experiences. Their stories enrich your life and help you see your own uniqueness in a new light.

3. **Step into the unknown.**

Push the boundaries of your comfort zone. Take risks, try something new, and embrace the possibility of failure. Growth lives on the other side of discomfort.

4. **Practice mindfulness.**

Slow down and savor the present moment. Release the need for control, and allow yourself to experience life in all its messy, unpredictable glory.

Life isn't a lab, and perfection is an illusion. By letting go of the impossible, we make room for the incredible. Embracing variation isn't just about accepting life as it is—it's about celebrating it. It's about seeing beauty in the mess, joy in the unexpected, and strength in resilience.

Let life surprise you. Let variation be your guide. You'll find that the path is richer, the connections deeper, and the possibilities endless.

11

YOUR INNER CIRCLE

"It's better to hang out with people better than you.
Pick out associates whose behavior is better than yours
and you'll drift in that direction."

—Warren Buffett

One of the most impactful books I've ever read is *Relational Intelligence* by Darius Daniels. This book opened my eyes to the way we interact with people in our lives and how we categorize those relationships. Daniels breaks it down into four key groups: friends, associates, assignments, and advocates. Understanding these categories has massively changed how I approach my relationships. This isn't about cutting people off, blocking or distancing yourself, but about knowing where everyone fits and how to manage those connections effectively.

Daniels makes an insightful reference to the Bible, pointing out that Yeshua had twelve disciples, but He was only truly close to three of them. That was intentional. He knew the value of each relationship but also recognized the need to be selective about where He placed His energy. The disciples all worked together, but that didn't mean they were all equally close.

This teaches us a valuable life lesson: you're going to encounter people in your life—whether at work or even in your own family—that you may not be particularly close to. And that's okay. What's important is knowing how much you share and invest in those relationships.

I had to learn this myself as I grew older. When I was younger, I had friends I was really close to people I hung out with regularly, but over time, I realized we didn't share the same goals. That didn't make them any less important to me, but I knew we were heading in different directions. This realization hit me hardest when I made the decision to go to college. Leaving the familiar streets, friends, and routines I had known for so long felt intimidating, especially as I stepped into an unfamiliar environment where I had to build new friendships from scratch.

I remember my neighbors telling me that when I returned from college, my friends would be where I left them, and they were right. Life had moved on for both me and them. It wasn't that they were bad friends; they just weren't chasing the same things I was chasing. My goals had shifted, and naturally, so did my circle. In college, I formed new friendships with people who shared similar ambitions—completing our degrees and starting successful careers. That was the goal, and for some of us, it was realized. Others found different paths that didn't require a college degree but were equally successful in their own right.

As life evolved, I had to learn how to categorize the people in my life. Who were my true friends, and who were my associates? Friends are the ones you can trust, and the relationship is built on reciprocity and shared energy. We pour into each other equally, and there's a mutual understanding that we've got each other's backs. Associates, on the other hand, are people you might know well but don't necessarily share intimate details of your life with. It's a different kind of relationship with less vulnerability.

Then there are assignments. These are people you're meant to guide, mentor, or provide support for without expecting anything in return. It's not about getting something from them—it's about helping them achieve their goals. I've had several mentees where my role was simply to give them the tools and direction to succeed, but they had to put in the work themselves. You don't expect anything back other than perhaps the satisfaction of seeing them thrive.

Finally, there are advocates—people who support you, sometimes without even having a close personal relationship. I've experienced this firsthand with my nonprofit, Illuminate STEM, and my podcast, The BlerdOut Movement. Some people championed my cause simply because they believed in what I was doing, even if we weren't particularly close. And that's a powerful thing to recognize—that advocacy doesn't always come from those you're personally invested in, but it can still make a huge impact.

Learning how to place people in these categories has been a game-changer for me. I've seen how it can bring clarity to relationships that might otherwise feel overwhelming or confusing. It's about knowing who fits where and understanding the role they play in your journey.

THE POWER OF INFLUENCE

We are profoundly shaped by the company we keep. It is often said that we are the sum of the five people we spend the most time with. These individuals influence our thoughts, behaviors, and beliefs in ways we may not always realize. From the moment we are born, we are surrounded by people who shape our development. Parents, siblings, friends, teachers, and colleagues all leave their mark on us. Their attitudes, behaviors, and values subtly—and sometimes overtly—mold our own. This reality underscores a profound truth: we must be mindful of the company we keep.

Consider the halo effect, a cognitive bias where our overall impression of a person influences our judgment of their specific traits. If someone close to us possesses a particularly admirable quality, such as confidence or kindness, we may unconsciously adopt and emulate that trait. This phenomenon highlights the importance of surrounding ourselves with individuals who exhibit the qualities we aspire to embody.

The power of proximity cannot be overstated. Those closest to us have the most significant impact on our lives. We are more likely to adopt their habits, share their beliefs, and align with their values. This proximity effect can either propel us toward our goals or hold us back, depending on the nature of these influences.

THE FIVE PEOPLE CLOSEST TO YOU

Let's dive deeper into the impact of the five people who are closest to you. These individuals can be friends, family, colleagues, mentors, or romantic partners. Each plays a unique role in shaping who you are.

FRIENDS

Friends are often our chosen family. They influence our behavior, attitudes, and even our worldview. A supportive friend can inspire us to pursue our dreams, while a negative one can drain our energy and enthusiasm. Choosing friends who uplift and encourage us is essential. They should push us to be the best versions of ourselves.

FAMILY

Family members, especially those we interact with regularly, profoundly influence our values and beliefs. They are our first teachers and role models. Their impact is deeply ingrained, often shaping our identity and guiding our moral compass. While we may not choose our family, we can choose how we interact with them and how much we allow their influence to shape our lives.

COLLEAGUES

Colleagues impact our work habits and professional attitudes. They can influence our motivation, performance, and career goals. A positive, ambitious work environment can drive us to achieve great things, while a toxic one can stifle our growth and creativity. It's crucial to seek out professional relationships that challenge us to grow and succeed.

MENTORS

Mentors provide guidance, support, and wisdom. They help us navigate our paths, offering insights based on their experiences. A good mentor can be a catalyst for personal and professional development, helping us achieve our goals and reach new heights. Seek mentors who inspire you and align with your aspirations.

ROMANTIC PARTNERS

Romantic partners profoundly affect our happiness, sense of self, and overall well-being. They provide emotional support, companionship, and motivation. A healthy, loving relationship can enhance our lives and help us thrive, while a toxic one can be detrimental. Choose a partner who supports your growth and shares your vision for the future.

HARNESSING THE POWER OF INFLUENCE

Understanding the power of influence allows us to harness it to improve our lives. Begin by choosing your circle wisely. Surround yourself with people who have a positive impact on you, who share your values, and who inspire you to be better. This intentional selection of your inner circle can significantly affect your personal and professional growth.

The power of influence is immense, shaping who we are and who we become. By being mindful of the company we keep, we can harness this power to elevate our lives and the lives of those around us. Surround yourself with individuals who inspire, support, and challenge you to grow. Model positive behavior and be aware of negative influences. Remember, you are the sum of the five people closest to you. Choose them wisely, and you'll find yourself on a path of continuous growth and fulfillment. Embrace the power of influence, and let it guide you toward a brighter, more prosperous future.

12

LEAD WITH LOGIC (NOT EMOTION)

"Character, not circumstances, makes the man."

—Booker T. Washington

As an engineer, logic is second nature to me.

I approach problems like they're math equations, analyzing every variable and calculating the best possible solution. If something doesn't make sense, I'm quick to point it out and explain why. This analytical mindset has served me well in many areas of my life, but it can be challenging when it comes to relationships—whether with family, friends, or colleagues. Logic doesn't always leave room for the gray areas where emotions live, and I've had to learn to balance the two.

One of the most valuable lessons I've learned in this regard comes from Stephen Covey's book, *The 7 Habits of Highly Effective People*, particularly Habit 5: "Seek first to understand, then to be understood." It's my favorite habit because it reminds me to reel myself in during challenging moments. Sometimes, people don't want solutions—they just want to be heard. They want someone to listen to them without judgment, to understand their feelings without immediately jumping to fix the problem.

There have been times when I've struggled with this balance, where I've let emotion take over when logic might have been the better guide—or vice versa. In moments of deep emotion, such as losing someone I cared about, I've had to learn that it's okay to step away from being the logical problem-solver and simply feel. Vulnerability, I've come to realize, is a superpower, not a weakness.

One of the most emotional times in my life was during my first year at Tennessee State University. My best friend Buddy passed away, and the loss hit me hard. I was ready to drop out of college, go back to Detroit, and give up on everything I had worked for. The logical part of me couldn't process the grief; it didn't have a solution for the pain I was feeling. But in that moment, it wasn't logic that saved me—it was the people around me.

My new friends at Tennessee State didn't know much about me, especially the things I kept hidden. But they saw my pain and responded with empathy and support. They didn't try to solve my problems; instead, they offered a listening ear and a shoulder to cry on. They showed me that it was okay to be vulnerable, to feel weak, and to not have all the answers. The next thing I knew, at 3 o'clock in the morning, my room-mates woke me up to make a rap album in the middle of the night. Our album "Live from 519" gave me an opportunity to express how I was feeling then and in the past through music. We made so much noise that night we woke up the 5th-floor RA and pretended like we were asleep when he came to our door at 5 am. The free expression and laughter were just what I needed to shake the pain. Their compassion helped me stay in school and move forward, even when I thought I couldn't.

This experience taught me the importance of leading with both logic and emotion, depending on the situation. While logic can guide us through many challenges, there are times when emotion needs to take the lead. When we allow ourselves to be vulnerable, we open up the possibility for deeper connections and greater understanding.

Now, when faced with emotional situations—whether it's my own grief or someone else's pain—I remind myself to turn off the "engineer logic" and simply be present. I strive to listen more, empathize, and offer support without immediately jumping to solutions. In doing so, I've learned that sometimes, the most logical thing we can do is to embrace our emotions and let them guide us to a place of healing and connection.

In the end, balancing logic and emotion isn't about choosing one over the other. It's about knowing when to lean on each understanding that both are essential to leading a full and meaningful life. Vulnerability, far from being a weakness, is what makes us human—and it's what allows us to connect with others on a deeper level.

THE DANGERS OF EMOTIONAL PROTESTING

In the heat of the moment, it's easy to let emotions take the lead. Injustices stir anger, sadness, or frustration, prompting immediate reactions to voice these feelings loudly. While such passion is understandable, it often leads to unintended consequences, including polarization. Emotional protests can widen the divide between opposing sides, making it harder to find common ground. This polarization entrenches people in their views, diminishing the likelihood of productive dialogue and meaningful compromise.

Misrepresentation is another risk of emotional protesting. High emotions can shift the focus from core issues to the expression of those emotions. Media and public narratives often interpret protests through the lens of their intensity rather than their purpose, distorting the understanding of the issues at hand and undermining the objectives of the protest.

Moreover, emotional protests can foster division within communities. Confrontational actions can create rifts among potential allies, weakening the collective strength needed to drive change. Internal conflicts divert energy from larger goals, impeding progress toward meaningful reform.

LEADING WITH LOGIC

Leading with logic doesn't mean suppressing emotions; it means channeling them constructively. Using objective data to support your cause is a powerful strategy. Facts and figures provide a solid foundation for arguments, making it harder for opponents to dismiss concerns as mere emotional outbursts. Objective data illustrates the scope of the problem and the necessity for change in a compelling and irrefutable manner.

Rational dialogue is another cornerstone of logical protesting. Conversations grounded in respect and understanding bridge gaps between differing viewpoints. Listening to opposing perspectives and responding thoughtfully fosters mutual respect and opens pathways to consensus. Rational dialogue humanizes issues, transforming them from abstract concepts into shared human concerns.

A balanced perspective is crucial when leading with logic. Acknowledging the complexities of issues and weighing the pros and cons of various solutions demonstrates maturity. This approach highlights a willingness to find viable, long-term solutions rather than resorting to quick fixes driven by emotion.

HOW TO LEAD (GENTLY) WITH LOGIC

Protesting with care involves mindfulness of triggers that elicit strong emotional responses. Recognizing these triggers enables protesters to remain calm and composed, even in heated situations. This mindfulness prevents conflicts from escalating and keeps the focus on core issues.

Self-awareness is another key aspect. Understanding one's own emotions and their influence on actions promotes objectivity. Self-awareness allows for measured, constructive responses rather than reactive ones.

Respectful dialogue is essential when engaging with others, especially those with opposing views. Treating others with kindness and empathy, even in disagreement, de-escalates tensions and fosters meaningful discussions. Respectful dialogue shows a commitment to valuing diverse perspectives and finding common ground.

Protesting is a vital tool for social and political change, but it must be approached with care and consideration. Leading with logic enhances the effectiveness of protests and fosters meaningful change. By leveraging objective data, engaging in rational dialogue, and maintaining a balanced perspective, protesters can craft compelling arguments that resonate with broader audiences. Protesting with care means being mindful of triggers, practicing self-awareness, and engaging in respectful dialogue.

Together, these strategies create a more inclusive and understanding society that values dialogue and compromise over polarization and division. Let us lead with logic, grounded in a passion for justice, and pave the way for a brighter, more equitable future.

13

STAND OUT

"You have a responsibility to seek to make your nation a better nation in which to live. You have a responsibility to seek to make life better for everybody. And so you must be involved in the struggle for freedom and justice."

—Dr. Martin Luther King

Standing out has never been my goal, but sometimes, it becomes necessary.

I'm not the kind of person who seeks attention just for the sake of it. I've always been content with doing my work, contributing to my community, and keeping a low profile. But there have been moments when I realized that standing out wasn't just about me—it was about something bigger, something that others needed to see.

One of those moments happened at the Automate conference, a major event for robotics and automation professionals. As I stood in the middle of the conference floor, I looked around and realized I was the only black man in a sea of thousands. There were other people of color, but as an engineer, I stood out even more. I was talking to a woman who was in sales, and as I looked around, it hit me. *This is your responsibility, Terrence.*

At that moment, I felt a shift. I had always been the person who did my work, mentored kids, and then went home to mind my business. But here, surrounded by thousands of people who didn't look like me, I felt an obligation to be seen, not for myself, but for the young people who might one day aspire to be where I was, who needed to know that someone like them could succeed in this field.

This realization led me to step out of my comfort zone and become more vocal about my work and my presence in the industry. It wasn't easy, and even now, I haven't fully embraced the spotlight the way I want to. The perfectionist in me always wants things to be just right before I put myself out there. But I've learned that sometimes, it's more important to just show up.

As I began to be more visible, people started to take notice. Articles were written, and people began to ask, "Do you know Terrence?" It was strange to see my name appear on multiple pages of Google search results to read about myself in ways I hadn't anticipated. But I was encouraged to own the moment, to accept that this was a part of my journey.

One day, a young man approached me and said, "I've been following you for years on LinkedIn—I'm trying to follow in your footsteps." It was a humbling experience, knowing that someone had been inspired by my work without me even realizing it. There are kids who've done book reports on me and students who've written papers about my career. It's a strange feeling to know that people are talking about you, and yet they still don't fully know the real you. But I've come to accept that they love who I am already, and that's okay.

Even the decision to write and publish this book is a form of standing out. It's a way of sharing stories that I've kept private, stories that have shaped who I am today. Yes, it was difficult growing up in Detroit. Yes, I've dealt with epilepsy, broken parents, and traumatic experiences like the bookmobile robbery that stole my innocence & shook my childhood. These are things most people don't know about me, but they're a part of my story, a part of what has made me who I am.

The Detroit Bookmobile was a safe haven for me, a little oasis parked in the heart of my neighborhood, filled with stories that transported me to worlds far from my reality. That day in 1985, my mom and I were only supposed to be returning a few books. As we stood in a line of other parents with their children, I was standing next to books near the entrance door when suddenly my head was snatched back, mouth covered, and a gun to my head. Startled by the silence, I looked at my mother and the other mothers with fear in their eyes; I stayed calm because I didn't want to be shot by anyone else. My heart pounded, and I froze as he barked orders, "Give me your money and jewelry, or I will shoot this kid," as the gun remained pressed to my head. The bookmobile was supposed to be a place of safety and the opportunity to be fed with knowledge, but at that moment, it had transformed into a prison. But nothing happened. I held my breath, watching as he took what he wanted, his presence swallowing the air, leaving us all paralyzed in fear. Then, in an instant, he was gone, leaving only silence—and the realization that I'd seen the darkness of the world up close, even within the walls of my childhood sanctuary. As we made it back home just a block away, my mother was still shaken and filled with tears. I was emotionless and filled with rage; I never cried. That was just the beginning of the unpredictable warpath I would go on.

Almost 40 years later, I read the front page article in the Detroit News about me and the bookmobile incident when I got curious enough to look up at the man who robbed the bookmobile. I was just seven years old at the time, and seeing his face on Facebook for the first time brought back a flood of memories. I didn't know what to think—should I be angry? Should I be grateful that he didn't shoot me? It was a reminder of how far I've come from that scared child to the person I am today.

People who read this book might be shocked to learn about some of the things I've been through, but I've realized that this is my moment to share those stories. I want to stand out, not just for myself but for those who need to see that it's possible to overcome even the most challenging circumstances.

Now, I have my own podcast where I share these stories where people can learn more about the journey that brought me here. It took time to get comfortable standing out and being the face of something larger than myself. But I've learned that sometimes standing out is not just about you— it's about giving others the courage to do the same.

ACKNOWLEDGE DIFFERENCES

Being in an environment where nobody looks like you can be both daunting and transformative. Imagine walking into a room and feeling all eyes on you, the unspoken weight of expectations and stereotypes pressing down. This moment, though challenging, is also a profound opportunity. It's your chance to redefine narratives, offer a fresh perspective, and demonstrate what true diversity and inclusion can achieve.

Together, let's delve into how to navigate these environments and stand out with confidence and grace.

The first step in thriving within a diverse environment is to acknowledge differences. Pretending that differences don't exist creates invisible walls that lead to tension and misunderstanding. Recognizing and respecting the unique backgrounds, experiences, and perspectives of others unlocks doors to genuine connections and meaningful growth. Acknowledging differences doesn't mean fixating on what separates us; instead, it's about celebrating the vibrant tapestry of diversity that surrounds us and finding strength within it.

Picture walking into a room where everyone speaks a different language. Initially, it feels isolating, even intimidating. But as you begin to learn their language and immerse yourself in their culture, common ground emerges. You start to appreciate their stories and contributions. This exchange of respect and curiosity fosters a sense of community and belonging, transcending the initial barriers.

To build this understanding, take active steps to learn about the cultures, traditions, and histories of those around you. Attend cultural events, read books, watch documentaries, or simply engage in heartfelt conversations. This not only broadens your own perspective but also shows respect for the richness others bring to the table. Cultural competency deepens relationships and enriches every interaction.

FIND ALLIES

In any environment, allies are essential. Allies are those individuals who share your values and stand by you in pursuit of your goals. They provide a sense of solidarity, amplifying your voice and helping you navigate challenges with greater ease. Finding allies isn't about gravitating toward people who mirror your identity. It's about connecting with those who recognize the value of diversity and are dedicated to fostering an inclusive atmosphere.

Seek out people who demonstrate a commitment to equity and understanding. These allies can offer support, share insights, and even open doors to new opportunities. Don't hesitate to share your own journey and experiences. Your story—with all its unique complexities—is a bridge that connects, educates, and inspires. Sharing your perspective helps dismantle stereotypes and creates a space for open dialogue and mutual understanding.

At the same time, listen deeply to others. Their stories hold invaluable lessons, shedding light on perspectives you may not have encountered before. This reciprocal exchange of experiences builds empathy and strengthens bonds, creating a foundation for enduring collaboration and support.

EMBRACE YOUR UNIQUE IDENTITY

The journey to standing out begins with embracing your unique identity. Resist the temptation to blend in or conform to societal expectations. Instead, celebrate the qualities that make you distinct. Your individuality is a source of strength and an asset to any environment you inhabit.

Visualize a quilt crafted from an array of diverse fabrics. Each piece—with its own color, pattern, and texture—is integral to the quilt's beauty and completeness. Likewise, your unique identity enhances the richness and depth of your environment. When you fully embrace and celebrate who you are, you inspire others to do the same.

Standing out isn't about seeking attention; it's about living authentically and contributing meaningfully. When you honor your identity, others are encouraged to see the value of diversity and inclusion. By showing up as your true self, you model courage, authenticity, and the transformative power of representation.

THRIVE AND INSPIRE

Navigating diverse environments is undoubtedly challenging, but it's also a fertile ground for growth and connection. By acknowledging differences, finding allies, learning from others, and fully embracing your identity, you can not only thrive but also leave an indelible mark on those around you. Remember to approach every situation with openness, respect, and a willingness to learn. Your journey isn't just about standing out—it's about building bridges, fostering understanding, and creating a more inclusive world.

Step into every room with confidence. Stand proud in your truth. Let your light shine, illuminating the path for others to follow.

14

EXPAND YOUR REACH

"Your network is your net worth."

—John C. Maxwell

In 2006, after a few years as a youth robotics coach, I realized something important about the students I worked with. The time I had to make an impact on their lives was limited. Depending on when I met them—whether as freshmen or later in high school—I only had a few years to guide them and, hopefully, inspire them to pursue careers in engineering. For those I met early, like the ninth graders, I had four full years to influence them before they went off to college. But for others, I only had a year or two, which made me rethink how I could make a more lasting impact.

It was then that I decided to start a middle school LEGO robotics team. The idea came to me after a career day at a school in Detroit, Michigan. As I was leaving, I mentioned to the school that they should consider starting a LEGO robotics team. The problem, they said, was funding. So, I took matters into my own hands, using my own money to buy a robot and a laptop, and with the help of teachers, we started a team. That first year, sixty kids tried out, but we could only start with thirty.

That's when I met two incredible young people who would forever change my experience as a mentor: James Meadows and Tia Smith. James was in the sixth grade, and Tia was just starting fourth grade. Little did I know at the time how special they would become—not just to the team but to me personally. I still mentor both of them to this day, and they've grown into remarkable adults.

James stood out from the very beginning. He was the last person I chose for the team, but not because he wasn't qualified. In fact, I picked him last on purpose, knowing how badly he wanted to be part of the robotics team. His teacher had told me how much it meant to him, and I wanted to challenge him. Even at twelve years old, he already had a clear vision for his future. When he was asked to write about his aspirations for another program, he wrote that he wanted to be a robotics engineer, just like me. I still have that letter, and it's a reminder of the importance of being present in a young person's life.

James quickly became one of my best students, but he also became the only student I ever had to remove from the team. As much as he wanted to be a robotics engineer, I held him to high standards, and when he didn't meet the GPA requirement I had set, I made the difficult decision to temporarily take him off the team. I told him he could come back if he brought his grades up, and to his credit, he did. But during his time off the team, I had to train someone else, and that's where Tia came in.

Tia was younger, but she stepped up to the challenge of becoming the team's lead robot programmer. She learned quickly and excelled, leading the team during one of the most pivotal moments of our journey. When James returned, the team worked together and ended up competing at the world championship in the RoboFest competition. We didn't win first place, but we took second, finishing just behind a team from Singapore. What really shook the room that day, though, was the sight of a group of young black kids competing—and excelling—in a field where they were the only ones who looked like them.

Today, both James and Tia are accomplished engineers. James fulfilled his dream of becoming a robotics engineer, and Tia is on her way to becoming a patent attorney. I'm proud to say that I've been with them every step of the way, from middle school to high school and college. I attended all of their graduations, and we still maintain a close mentor-mentee relationship. They are both living proof of what can happen when you invest time, effort, and belief in young people.

Starting that middle school LEGO team was one of the best decisions I ever made. It gave me more time to guide students like James and Tia, starting them on the right path earlier in life. By the time they reached high school, we had built a strong foundation, and that mentorship continued through college and beyond. These relationships are more than just professional connections; they are lifelong bonds, and I couldn't be prouder of what they've accomplished.

DEVELOP YOUR EXPERTISE

Influence. It's a powerful force. Each of us possesses it to some degree, but the ability to harness, expand, and wield it wisely can profoundly shape our lives and the lives of others. Influence isn't just about having a voice—it's about making that voice resonate deeply and meaningfully.

Becoming an expert in your field is the cornerstone of influence. People are drawn to those who command knowledge and inspire confidence. Expertise isn't given; it's earned. It demands dedication, relentless curiosity, and an ongoing commitment to learning. Imagine being a trusted source—a beacon of clarity and guidance in a sea of uncertainty. That's the power of true expertise.

To cultivate this level of mastery, immerse yourself fully in your chosen field. Read voraciously, attend workshops, seek mentorship, and engage with thought leaders. Knowledge is powerful, but applied knowledge is transformative. Share your insights—write articles, deliver talks, and teach others. The more you contribute, the more you amplify your influence. Expertise enables you to help others, and in doing so, you expand your reach and impact.

BUILD YOUR NETWORK

Influence doesn't grow in isolation. A strong, supportive network is essential. Surround yourself with like-minded individuals who challenge and inspire you. Attend industry events, join professional organizations, and participate in online communities. These connections will not only broaden your reach but also provide invaluable support, insights, and resources.

Networking is about more than collecting contacts; it's about building meaningful relationships. Authenticity is key. Approach every interaction with sincerity and a willingness to give. Offer your help freely, and you'll find others more willing to reciprocate. True influence stems from actions, not words. Be the kind of person others admire and respect by leading with integrity and consistency.

Leadership by example means embodying the values you want to see in the world. When people witness your authenticity and commitment, they're more likely to trust and follow you. Integrity builds trust, and trust is the bedrock of influence. People are inspired by those who stand firm in their principles and lead with purpose.

LEVERAGE SOCIAL MEDIA

In today's digital world, social media is an unparalleled tool for expanding your reach. Platforms like Twitter, LinkedIn, and Instagram offer a stage for your voice to be heard by a global audience. But effective use of social media goes beyond broadcasting your message; it's about fostering genuine connections and meaningful conversations.

Create content that educates, inspires, and resonates with your audience. Share insights, highlight pressing issues, and celebrate success stories. Engage actively by responding to comments, joining discussions, and showing gratitude for your community. Social media isn't just a megaphone—it's a dialogue. By nurturing your online presence, you can amplify your influence and make a lasting impact far beyond your immediate network.

COLLABORATE FOR GREATER IMPACT

Collaboration is the multiplier of influence. When you join forces with others, you combine strengths, resources, and perspectives, creating something greater than the sum of its parts. Seek opportunities to partner with individuals and organizations that align with your values and vision.

Collaboration fuels innovation by blending diverse ideas and experiences. It fosters creativity, uncovers fresh solutions, and extends your reach. Working together with others allows you to achieve goals that would be unattainable alone. As you build coalitions and drive collective action, your influence expands exponentially.

THE TRUE POWER OF INFLUENCE

Expanding your reach isn't just about being heard; it's about being effective, credible, and authentic. Develop expertise, cultivate meaningful relationships, lead with integrity, harness the power of social media, and embrace collaboration. Influence is a tool of immense potential—when guided by wisdom and purpose, it can ignite meaningful change.

Remember, influence is not about power or control. It's about creating a positive ripple effect in the world. Use your influence to inspire, educate, and uplift. Help others achieve their dreams, and in turn, you'll realize your own. This is the true essence of influence: to let your light shine brightly and empower others to do the same.

15

GUARD YOUR HEART

"Resentment is like drinking poison and then hoping it will kill your enemies."

—Nelson Mandela

Guarding my heart has been a crucial part of my journey. Over the years, I've learned to protect myself from people who try to remind me of my past—as if my mistakes and experiences should define who I am today. It's a challenge, but I've grown strong enough to confront those moments with the understanding that yesterday's price is not today's price. The past is behind me, and I have the power to shape my present and future without being held back by what once was.

One of the most important lessons I've learned is that people will sometimes use your past as leverage against you. They'll weaponize your history, attempting to pull you back into an identity you've outgrown. To guard my heart, I've had to trust myself and remember that I've overcome those challenges. I've moved forward, and there's no reason to look back in fear or shame. It's a daily battle, but one that I'm determined to win.

A pivotal moment in my journey came during a therapy session. My therapist suggested I ask a close friend what they found beautiful about me. When I did, their response caught me off guard. They mentioned that when I shared stories about my high school life and childhood in Detroit, it seemed like I was running from myself during my college years. That hit me hard. I realized they were right—I had been running from my past, trying to escape the version of myself that I no longer wanted to be.

This internal struggle created two versions of me: "Little Terrence," the person I was trying to leave behind, and "Big Terrence," the person I was striving to become. Little Terrence had always been a protector, especially when life got tough. He was young, radical, and sometimes violent, quick to react with anger and defensiveness. When someone said something that triggered me, Little Terrence would come out swinging, ready to defend at all costs. But over time, I realized that these reactions were doing more harm than good.

Reacting in anger or defensiveness only served to strengthen the very things I was trying to escape. My emotional outbursts became signs of weakness, reminders that I hadn't fully dealt with the issues from my past. I began to understand that my silence, my ability to hold back and not react, could be far more powerful than any outburst. It was a sign of growth, of moving beyond the triggers that once controlled me.

This process of guarding my heart is ongoing. It's like trying to walk past a Reese's cup without grabbing it—something that's not easy for me! But the day I can do it, the day I can walk past without giving in to temptation, I know I've made progress. Similarly, when I can face reminders of my past without being triggered, I know I'm winning the battle to guard my heart.

Forming these habits, breaking old ones, and learning new ways to respond have been crucial. People often react out of habit because they don't know another way. But I'm glad to say that today, I know better. I've learned how to combat those moments, to protect my heart from being pulled back into a place I no longer belong.

Guarding my heart is about more than just resisting negative influences—it's about nurturing the strength within me to keep moving forward. It's about recognizing that I am not defined by my past but by the choices I make today. And every day that I choose to protect my heart, to trust myself, and to silence the voices that try to drag me back, I become a stronger, more resilient version of myself.

WHEN YOU'VE BEEN HURT BEFORE

Life's journey is full of connections, and with those connections comes vulnerability. We let people in, hoping for mutual respect and care, but sometimes the result is pain. In those moments, guarding your heart becomes essential—not as a means of shutting the world out, but as an act of wisdom and self-preservation. Guarding your heart means being intentional about who you trust and how much of yourself you choose to share. It's about creating space for meaningful relationships while protecting your emotional well-being.

When you've been hurt before, the instinct to shield yourself from further pain is only natural. But don't let fear be the gatekeeper of your heart. Healing is a process, and it begins with self-compassion. Acknowledge your wounds and give yourself time to recover. Rebuild your sense of trust, first in yourself and then in others. While not everyone will honor your trust, there are people who will cherish it. When you're ready, step forward with caution but also with hope.

Imagine a garden after a storm. The petals may be scattered and the stems bent, but with care and attention, the garden can bloom again. Similarly, your heart can flourish. Guarding it isn't about locking it away; it's about nurturing it until it's strong enough to welcome the right people.

WHEN YOU'RE DEALING WITH A TOXIC PERSON

Toxic individuals can infiltrate our lives, bringing chaos, negativity, and pain. They might manipulate, belittle, or drain you, leaving you feeling diminished. Guarding your heart against such people isn't just wise—it's necessary. Limiting your exposure to their harmful behavior or removing them from your life entirely is an act of self-respect and survival.

Picture toxic people as weeds in a flourishing garden. Left unchecked, they strangle the life out of vibrant flowers. By uprooting the weeds, you make room for beauty to thrive. Similarly, removing toxic influences creates space for you to grow, heal, and rediscover your strength.

Guarding your heart doesn't mean building walls. It means recognizing what drains your spirit and having the courage to protect your inner peace. The act of stepping away from toxicity is not a rejection of others but an affirmation of your worth.

WHEN YOU'RE NOT SURE ABOUT SOMEONE

Life often presents us with new relationships that feel uncertain. Some people seem genuine but may not yet have earned your trust. In these moments, guarding your heart means giving time the opportunity to reveal your true intentions. It's not about suspicion—it's about prudence.

Think of a seedling. You wouldn't expect it to grow into a sturdy tree overnight. It needs nurturing, sunlight, and patience. Trust, like that seedling, thrives when allowed to grow gradually. Don't rush it. Let trust prove itself through consistent actions, not just words.

It's okay to take your time. Use discernment as your guide, and let relationships evolve naturally. Remember, trust is a gift—not something to be given lightly.

BE MINDFUL OF WHO YOU LET INTO YOUR LIFE

Your inner circle shapes your emotional and mental landscape. Be intentional about who you invite into that sacred space. Pay attention to people's actions—consistency and reliability are the cornerstones of trust. Words can be persuasive, but actions reveal the truth.

Building trust is like constructing a home. You wouldn't hire unskilled workers to lay the foundation. Similarly, surround yourself with people who are dependable and genuine. Healthy relationships are built on mutual respect, shared values, and unwavering support.

Establishing boundaries is essential for protecting your heart. Boundaries don't shut people out; they define how you expect to be treated. They're a sign of self-respect, not hostility. Imagine boundaries as a fence around your garden— not to block beauty but to shield it from harm. Communicate your boundaries clearly and enforce them with courage. The people who value you will honor them.

TAKE CARE OF YOURSELF

Your well-being is the foundation of your strength. Prioritize self-care—nurture your mind, body, and spirit. Engage in activities that bring you joy, fulfillment, and peace. Self-care isn't indulgent; it's essential. When you invest in yourself, you cultivate resilience for life's challenges.

Think of self-care as tending to your garden. Without water and sunlight, even the most beautiful flowers will wither. By prioritizing your well-being, you create a thriving environment for growth, allowing you to embrace life's highs and weather its lows with grace.

A BALANCED APPROACH TO GUARDING YOUR HEART

Guarding your heart is about balance. It's not about closing off but about opening wisely. Trust is a treasure, and you hold the key to determining who is worthy of it. Set boundaries, embrace self-care, and allow yourself to grow stronger. Protect your heart not out of fear but out of love— for yourself and for the life you're building.

Guard your heart like a precious garden. With careful tending, it will bloom, not just for your benefit but for those who are fortunate enough to walk beside you. Trust is the bridge between protection and connection. Build it thoughtfully, and it will lead to relationships that nourish your soul.

16

FIND YOUR "ANGER TRANSLATOR"

"You can't separate peace from freedom because no one can be at peace unless he has his freedom."

—Malcolm X.

Anger is a powerful force.

Besides love, there's no more powerful motivation inside of us. Millions of people have let their anger destroy their lives and those of the people they love most. And millions more people than that have been traumatized by the anger of another person directed at us.

But the fact is this: anger doesn't have to be destructive.

For many years, I struggled with how to handle my anger. On the inside, I often felt a fiery intensity, but I rarely let it show on the outside. Instead, I channeled it into a calm, controlled demeanor. This wasn't always easy, but it became a crucial part of my personal and professional growth.

I think back to my early days as a young engineer, working under my mentor, Ray Roberts. Ray was the fiery version of me—always passionate, always intense. He often commended me for being more relaxed and calm than he was. But what he didn't realize was that on the inside, I felt just as intense as he did. The difference was that I expressed it differently. I learned to let my anger fuel me in a way that came out smoothly and intentionally rather than explosively.

This ability to control my emotions and channel my anger into something productive has been one of the most beneficial skills I've developed. It's allowed me to navigate difficult situations with a clear head and a steady hand. In relationships, for example, people often equate a calm demeanor with a lack of care. They assume that if I'm not visibly upset, I must not be invested in the situation. But what I've come to understand is that true control over my emotions doesn't mean I care any less—it means I'm able to approach challenges with clarity and purpose.

Ever seen the comedy duo *Key & Peele*? They have an episode where President Obama (played by Jordan Peele) gives a calm, composed speech, while his sidekick Luther (played by Keegan-Michael Key) serves as his "anger translator," expressing the President's repressed frustrations in a more blunt, exaggerated, and emotional way. It's hilarious. The skit plays on the contrast between how Obama was perceived to be calm and diplomatic, while Luther externalizes the raw emotions he (and many of us) might suppress when talking about certain things.

I think this concept can be applied to our own lives when dealing with anger. Like Obama in the sketch, we often need to maintain composure, especially in professional or tense situations, while internally feeling a range of emotions. However, finding a "translator" for our own emotions—whether it's through journaling, talking to a trusted friend, or practicing mindfulness—can help us release those feelings without causing harm or escalation. The key takeaway is learning to balance emotional expression with self-control, making sure we deal with anger in a healthy way while still acknowledging and processing it.

In a sense, we all have an "anger translator" within us—how we choose to channel that can determine whether we handle situations with grace and control or let our frustrations get the better of us.

No, when it comes to leadership, this control is even more crucial. When you're leading others, they look to you for guidance and stability. They don't want to see someone who's easily rattled, someone who lets their emotions dictate their actions. They want a leader who can stand in front of a crowd and speak with confidence, guiding them toward a common goal. Screaming and yelling may release pent-up anger, but it rarely achieves anything productive. Instead, it often leads to more chaos, more confusion, and less progress.

Over time, I've learned to ask myself a simple question in moments of anger: *What do I want to achieve from this?* Going into a situation fueled by anger without a clear goal in mind is like expecting a storm to produce sunshine. You can't create something positive from a place of rage. But if you approach it with control, with a clear intention, you can turn that anger into a force for good.

I've come to see my ability to channel anger as a form of self-trust. I trust myself to say the right things, to use the right tone, and to achieve my goals without needing to be forceful or aggressive. It's like knowing how to handle fire—if you let it rage uncontrolled, it can destroy everything in its path. But if you learn to manage it and use it wisely, it can provide warmth, light, and energy.

In the end, learning to control my emotions has allowed me to transform anger into strength. It's given me the ability to face challenges with confidence and to lead others with calm assurance. By trusting myself to handle anger constructively, I've been able to turn what could be a destructive force into a powerful tool for growth and progress.

ACKNOWLEDGE YOUR EMOTIONS

We all know the feeling. Anger bubbles up inside, demanding release, yet the words to express it elude us. You long to be heard, to be understood, but fear your anger might inflict more harm than healing. The frustration of miscommunication can be overwhelming. That's where your anger translator comes in. It's the inner voice that takes your raw emotions and shapes them into words others can understand. Developing this voice requires introspection, courage, and practice.

The first step in discovering your anger translator is to acknowledge your emotions. It's okay to feel angry, frustrated, or upset. These emotions are natural responses to life's challenges. Instead of suppressing them, sit with them. Ask yourself: where are these feelings coming from? By acknowledging your emotions, you validate your experiences and create a foundation for honest communication.

Imagine being caught in a storm. The wind howls, and the rain lashes down. You can't ignore it, but you can seek shelter and observe. Similarly, acknowledge your emotions. Don't run from them. Find a safe space within yourself to explore their origin. This awareness is the first step in transforming anger into words that resonate.

IDENTIFY YOUR TRIGGERS

Once you've acknowledged your emotions, take time to identify your triggers. What situations or interactions ignite your anger? Understanding these triggers prepares you to manage them constructively. Think of it as mapping a terrain before embarking on a journey. Knowing the potential pitfalls allows you to navigate more effectively.

Reflect on the last time you felt angry. What set it off? Was it a specific person, a situation, or perhaps an unmet expectation? Identifying triggers isn't about blaming others; it's about gaining insight into what affects you. This understanding empowers you to respond thoughtfully instead of reacting impulsively.

PRACTICE MINDFULNESS

Mindfulness is the practice of being fully present and engaged with your thoughts and emotions. It allows you to observe your anger without judgment, giving you the clarity to choose a healthier response. By practicing mindfulness, you can better understand your emotions and express them more effectively.

Picture mindfulness as tuning into a clear radio signal amidst static. It brings clarity, helping you decode your feelings and translate them into meaningful communication. Mindfulness can be nurtured through meditation, deep breathing, or simply paying attention to the present moment.

GIVE YOURSELF PERMISSION TO SPEAK

Expressing anger can feel daunting. You may fear being dismissed or hurting someone's feelings. But you deserve to speak your truth. Your feelings and experiences are valid. Imagine standing on a stage, poised and confident, addressing an attentive audience. That's how you should approach your emotions—with assurance and intention.

Speaking your truth isn't about causing harm; it's about fostering understanding. When you communicate honestly and thoughtfully, you invite connection rather than conflict. Remember, your voice matters. Your perspective is essential.

PRACTICE ACTIVE LISTENING

Effective communication is a two-way exchange. While expressing your emotions is vital, so is listening to others. Active listening involves fully engaging with the other person's words and seeking to understand their perspective. This mutual exchange builds respect and fosters understanding.

Think of communication as a dance. Two partners move in harmony, responding to each other's cues. By listening actively and responding thoughtfully, you create a balanced and meaningful dialogue. This approach ensures your anger is not just heard but truly understood.

SEEK SUPPORT

Finding your anger translator isn't always easy. It's okay to seek support. Trusted friends, family members, or therapists can provide a listening ear and offer constructive feedback. They can help you navigate your emotions and refine your communication strategies.

Think of support as a lighthouse guiding you through turbulent seas. It provides direction and reassurance. Surround yourself with people who understand your journey and offer encouragement. Their insights can be invaluable as you learn to communicate your emotions effectively.

EMBRACE THE JOURNEY

Finding your anger translator is about learning to communicate your emotions in a way that fosters connection and understanding. By acknowledging your feelings, identifying your triggers, and practicing mindfulness, you lay the groundwork for meaningful expression. Give yourself permission to speak your truth, practice active listening, and lean on your support system when needed.

Your emotions are valid. Your voice matters. By embracing this journey, you enhance your relationships and promote personal growth. Trust in your ability to communicate effectively. Let your voice ring clear and strong, transforming anger into a force that builds bridges instead of walls.

17

FATHERHOOD WITH NO BLUEPRINT

"You don't have to be perfect,
but you do have to be present."

—Denzel Washington

B ecoming a father has been the most rewarding and vulnerable journey of my life.

Growing up in a single-parent household, I didn't have a clear blueprint on how to be a dad. I had to learn on my own, drawing inspiration from the men I admired—my mentor Ray Roberts, Mr. Johnson, and others who were fathers and husbands. They became my models, even though they didn't know it. I observed how they led their families and how assertive yet compassionate they were, and I took notes. I also learned from fathers I didn't want to emulate, shaping my own approach to fatherhood.

Being a mentor to other kids before becoming a father myself gave me some confidence. Those kids looked up to me, and many of them, now adults, still tell me that I was a lot of fun, the kind of person they'd trust to watch their own children. But becoming a father to my daughter, Zorah, was different. It wasn't just about being fun or a good mentor. It was about modeling what it meant to be a strong, caring, and reliable presence in her life.

I've always been hard on myself about being the best father I can be. Growing up without my father's consistent presence made me determined to be there for Zorah in every way possible. I wanted to be strong for her, never showing any weakness. But over time, I realized that this wasn't realistic or healthy. One day, she noticed me crying due to a situation that brought me a great deal of pain. Initially, I tried to clean myself up, but then I thought, *No, let her see this.* I didn't want to hide my true emotions from her. As my daughter, she should see the real me—both my strengths and my vulnerabilities.

This decision to be vulnerable with her has strengthened our relationship. Now, when I'm having a tough day, I can tell her, "I'm not doing okay today," and she understands. She's learned to be patient, to wait when I need a moment, and to recognize that not every day is going to be perfect. This has made her a more understanding and empathetic child.

There have been other challenges, too. A few years ago, my daughter and I were attacked by a dog. It was a terrifying experience. For a long time after, Zorah was afraid of big dogs. It took years for her to feel comfortable around them again. But through it all, she trusted that her dad would always protect her—it might sound silly, but this experience was something that turned into a powerful bond of trust between us. That trust is something I've worked hard to build, and it's one of the most important aspects of being a father.

I've also had to navigate the complexities of explaining the world to her. As she grows older, her questions become more challenging. She recently asked me, "Why do people lie? Why not just tell the truth?" I had to pause and think about how to explain something so complex to a ten-year-old in a way that's sensitive and age-appropriate. I told her that most people are afraid that others will see their fears, so they lie to deflect from people learning the truth. Her curiosity is a reflection of my own, and now I have the responsibility to help her shape that curiosity in a constructive way.

Being a father means more than just protecting your child. It means being honest with them, showing them who you are, and guiding them through life's challenges. It means trusting yourself to make the right decisions, even when you don't have a perfect example to follow. Sometimes, it means apologizing when I make mistakes because we are not always *right* as parents.

If I could do it all over again, I would choose to be just as vulnerable as Zorah. It's this openness that has created the strong bond we share today. She asks big questions because she knows I'll give her thoughtful answers. She trusts me because I've shown her my true self, not just the strong, invincible dad, but the human being with emotions and challenges.

Trusting myself as a father has been a journey, but it's one that has taught me the value of vulnerability, the importance of being present, and the power of showing my daughter that it's okay to be real. And for that, I'm grateful every day.

HIGH EXPECTATIONS, RESILIENCE, AND CONFIDENCE

From the moment Zorah was old enough to understand, I made it clear that she was destined for greatness. Some might say it's too much pressure for a child, but I believe that setting high expectations is the foundation for success. When Zorah was preparing for her school's orbital test, I didn't just tell her to do her best—I told her to win. I wanted her to walk into that room with the confidence of a champion, already knowing she would come out on top.

The way we approach challenges in life is often a reflection of the mindset we develop in childhood. By setting high expectations, I'm teaching Zorah that she is capable of achieving anything she sets her mind to. This isn't about being the best in comparison to others; it's about being the best version of herself.

Life is full of ups and downs, and one of the most important lessons I can teach Zorah is how to bounce back from setbacks. Resilience isn't just a buzzword—it's a critical life skill. When Zorah encounters challenges, I don't shield her from them. Instead, I encourage her to face them head-on, knowing that she has the strength and intelligence to overcome any obstacle. Resilience is built through experience, and the best way for Zorah to learn it is by facing difficulties and learning how to navigate them. Whether it's a tough math problem or a disagreement with a friend, I guide her through the process of problem-solving, always reminding her that setbacks are temporary and that she has the power to turn them into opportunities for growth.

LEADING BY EXAMPLE AND ENCOURAGING INDEPENDENCE

Children learn more from what we do than what we say, and Zorah is no exception. I strive to be the best version of myself because I know she is watching. Whether it's in my work as an engineer, my role as a mentor, or simply how I treat others, I make sure that my actions align with the values I want to instill in her. I also give her access to hold me accountable for how I show up.

Zorah sees me as her superhero, and that means I have a responsibility to live up to that image. I show up for her, not just physically but emotionally and mentally. I want her to see that success is not just about achieving goals but also about how we handle ourselves in the process. By being present and engaged, I'm teaching her the importance of integrity, hard work, and compassion.

As much as I guide Zorah, I also encourage her to think for herself. Critical thinking is a skill that will serve her throughout her life, and it's one that I'm committed to developing in her. When she won the orbital test at school, it wasn't just because of the practice sessions we had together—it was because she took ownership of her preparation and believed in her ability to succeed.

Teaching Zorah to be independent doesn't mean leaving her to figure everything out on her own. It means giving her the tools and support she needs to make informed decisions and then stepping back to let her take the lead. This approach helps her build confidence in her judgment and prepares her to navigate the complexities of life.

NURTURING, REALISM, AND RESPONSIBILITY

Parenting is often a balancing act between nurturing and preparing our children for the realities of life. While I want to protect Zorah from the harshness of the world, I also know that shielding her too much could leave her unprepared. I make it a point to have honest conversations with her about the challenges she might face, whether in school, in friendships, or later in her career.

These discussions are not meant to scare her but to equip her with the resilience and critical thinking she will need to succeed. Life isn't always easy, and the sooner she understands that, the better prepared she will be to handle whatever comes her way.

Responsibility and accountability are cornerstones of Zorah's upbringing. From a young age, I've taught her the importance of taking responsibility for her actions and understanding the consequences of her choices. Whether it's something as simple as cleaning up after herself or as complex as managing her time effectively, Zorah knows that she is accountable for her actions.

This sense of responsibility extends to her academic and personal life. She knows that her success is largely in her own hands and that she has the power to shape her future. By instilling these values, I'm helping her develop into a responsible and capable adult.

CELEBRATING ACHIEVEMENTS AND SUPPORTING CREATIVITY

Every achievement, big or small, is celebrated in our home. When Zorah accomplishes something, I make sure she knows how proud I am of her. This positive reinforcement builds her self-esteem and motivates her to keep striving for excellence. But just as important as celebrating her victories is helping her learn from her failures.

I don't sugarcoat failure; instead, I teach Zorah that it's a natural part of life and an opportunity to learn and grow. When she falls short of a goal, we talk about what went wrong and how she can improve next time. This approach helps her develop a growth mindset, where challenges are seen as opportunities rather than obstacles.

Creativity is a key component of Zorah's development, and I do everything I can to encourage it. I want Zorah to understand that she has the power to create something meaningful and impactful. Whether this book turns into a TV show, a toy, or simply a cherished memory, the process of creating it is what matters most. It's about showing her that her ideas have value and that, with hard work and imagination, she can bring them to life.

INVOLVEMENT IN EDUCATION AND PREPARING FOR THE FUTURE

My involvement in Zorah's education goes beyond just helping with homework or attending parent-teacher conferences. I see education as a holistic process that includes academic learning, life skills, and emotional development. We practice for tests together, discuss what she's learning in school, and explore how it applies to the real world.

Education is not just about getting good grades. It's about preparing her for the future. I want Zorah to be a lifelong learner who is curious about the world and eager to expand her knowledge. By being actively involved in her education, I'm helping to instill a love of learning that will stay with her throughout her life.

As a parent, my ultimate goal is to prepare Zorah for a future where she can thrive independently and interdependently. This means equipping her with the skills, values, and mindset she needs to navigate life's challenges and seize its opportunities. Parenting is not just about providing for our children's needs today—it's about preparing them for the world they will face tomorrow.

In raising Zorah, I've learned that the most important gift I can give her is the belief in her own potential. By setting high expectations, teaching resilience, being a role model, and encouraging her creativity, I'm helping her build a foundation for a successful and fulfilling life. Parenting is a journey, and while there are no guarantees, I know that the lessons we've learned together will serve her well as she steps into the future.

18

SHARE YOUR STORY

"When you stand and share your story in an empowering way, your story will heal you, and your story will heal somebody else."

—Iyanla Vanzant.

Maya Angelou once wrote, "There is no greater agony than bearing an untold story inside you." It appears in her 1969 autobiography, *I Know Why the Caged Bird Sings*. This suggests that holding on to a story can be painful, but sharing it can be a path to healing and freedom. Sharing a story can be as simple as confiding in a loved one or therapist. It can also inspire and encourage others who may be going through similar struggles.

I can attest to this fact. The first time I stood in front of a large crowd to share my personal story felt surreal.

I had never imagined myself in that position—being the one at the podium, tasked not with delivering a lecture on robotics or mentoring but with opening up about my life.

The request came unexpectedly. It was Mr. Douglas, a good friend I'd only recently met, who made the call. "Hey, Terrence, the college wants you to speak at their summer graduation," he said. "But they don't want you to talk about engineering. They want you to share your story—your personal journey."

I paused, unsure. I had never spoken publicly about my life before—at least not in a way that made me vulnerable. My career as a robotics engineer? Sure, I could talk about that all day. But my personal life? That was uncharted territory. I told Mr. Douglas I'd need time to pray and think it over. He understood but mentioned the chancellor would be reaching out soon to confirm. It took all the nerve I had, but eventually, I agreed.

When the day came, I stood backstage, waiting for my turn. The nerves were almost too much. But as I stepped in front of that crowd of fresh-faced graduates, I decided to ease the tension with a joke. I told them about the first time I dunked a basketball when I was just twelve or thirteen. I was about 5'6" at the time—but I was determined. I figured out a way to throw myself an alley-oop, calculating every move down to the inches I needed to clear the rim and sink the ball. As I described it, I saw the amazement in their eyes. The story broke the ice, not just with the audience but with myself, too.

Then, I opened up. I talked about my childhood, growing up in a single-parent household, and the challenges I faced along the way. I shared the risks I had to take and the obstacles I overcame to be standing where I was. I wanted them to know that success wasn't always linear, and it wasn't out of their reach. I wasn't sure how they would respond, but when I finished, something remarkable happened.

At least ten young men and women approached me after my speech. "Mr. Southern," they said, "I grew up just like you. I went through the same struggles." Their gratitude floored me. Some of those students even became my mentees that day, and watching them grow into successful adults has been one of the greatest rewards of my life.

That day, I learned a powerful lesson: the importance of showing up and sharing your story, even when it feels uncomfortable. I almost didn't do it, but I'm glad I did, not just for me but for those young people whose lives were touched in ways I hadn't anticipated. That moment was the start of something special—my journey as a speaker and, more importantly, a mentor. I didn't know the impact I would have when I walked on that stage, but I'm thankful I found the courage to share and that I didn't cheat those students out of the message they needed to hear.

THE STORY WITHIN

We all carry stories within us, shaped by joy, pain, triumphs, and failures. Yet, too often, we hesitate to share them. Maybe we fear judgment or worry our experiences aren't significant. But the truth is, your story holds the potential to inspire, educate, and uplift others in ways you might never expect.

Vulnerability is the bridge between isolation and connection. When you share your authentic self, you invite others to do the same. Think about a time when someone opened up to you about their struggles or triumphs. Did it not create a bond of understanding? That's the magic of storytelling—it erases the distance between us, fostering empathy and trust.

BECOMING THE MIRROR

When you share your story, you become a mirror for others. Your journey—your victories and defeats—can help someone else see themselves more clearly. It might give them the courage to confront their fears or the strength to persevere through a difficult season.

Imagine someone feeling isolated, thinking their struggles are unique. Hearing your story might be the lifeline they need, a reminder that they are not alone. Your words can offer hope, resilience, and the belief that brighter days are ahead.

THE GIFT OF HEALING

Sharing your story doesn't just benefit others—it transforms you, too. It allows you to process your experiences, release shame, and embrace healing. It's like journaling but with the added power of human connection. Speaking your truth aloud can be liberating, helping you reclaim your narrative and find clarity.

Through vulnerability, you also build trust and authenticity. People are drawn to those who are unafraid to show their true selves. This authenticity fosters community—a network of people who see you, understand you and stand beside you.

OVERCOMING FEAR

Of course, sharing your story isn't easy. Fear of judgment can feel paralyzing. But remember: your story is a gift.

The impact it has on others far outweighs the discomfort of vulnerability. Focus on the lives you might touch rather than the criticism you might receive.

LET YOUR STORY BE HEARD

Your story matters. It's a thread in the larger tapestry of humanity, woven with lessons, hope, and wisdom. By sharing it, you contribute to a world where empathy, understanding, and trust can thrive.

So, trust the process. Trust yourself. And when the moment comes, step forward and let your voice be heard. You may be surprised by how deeply your story resonates—and by the lives it transforms, including your own.

A LETTER TO MY YOUNGER SELF

I see you, standing at the crossroads of uncertainty, grappling with fear and self-doubt. The ground beneath you feels like it's shifting, and the path forward is clouded by the unknown. But let me assure you, the strength you need to navigate this moment already resides within you.

I know you struggle to trust anyone, and for good reason. The betrayals and disappointments you've faced make that hard. But holding on to that distrust will only weigh you down in the long run. Trusting yourself is where your journey begins.

Trust not just the version of you who seems to know what to do, but also the one who doesn't—the one still figuring it out. Trust your instincts, your voice, and your ability to rise, even when things feel impossibly heavy. Life will test this trust repeatedly. People will betray you. You will be lied on. Some will try to take what is yours, and there will be losses. But hear me clearly: in the end, you will win. So keep going. Keep trusting yourself.

Uncertainty isn't your enemy; it's your greatest teacher. It will show you how to adapt, how to ask better questions, and how to sit with the discomfort of not knowing until clarity reveals itself. Resilience isn't just about bouncing back—it's about standing steady and refusing to give up, even when the winds of doubt try to knock you down.

You don't need to have it all figured out. You just need to take the next step, and then the next. Mistakes are part of the process, not signs of failure. Be patient with yourself and embrace the lessons that come your way. Deep down, I know you're not afraid of failing. You're afraid of succeeding beyond your wildest dreams—and that's okay.

Never forget: the very act of showing up, even when uncertainty looms, is proof of your courage. You are far more capable than you believe, and the future you're building will be a testament to the strength you're cultivating now.

Finally, thank you. Thank you for the unimaginable strength, perseverance, and resolve you've shown to bring me to where I am today. I could not have done this without you. But now it's time for you to rest. You've carried me this far, and I will take it from here.

With love and unshakable faith,

Terrence

ACKNOWLEDGMENTS

Writing this book has been a journey of trust itself, and I am deeply grateful to the many people who have walked this path with me. This process forced me to slow down, reflect, and draw out what was in my heart and what needed to be poured into these pages.

To my daughter, Zorah: You are the gift I never expected, but you continue to push me to greater heights every day. I take immense pride in being your father and hold myself accountable to show up as my best self—not just for you, but for us both.

To my family and friends: Thank you for your unwavering belief in me, even during moments when I doubted myself. Your love and support have been the foundation upon which my trust has grown. Your encouragement, patience, and thoughtful conversations have served as a compass, guiding me through uncharted territory.

To my mentors, teachers, and coaches: Your wisdom and guidance have been invaluable. You've shown me the power of trusting not only others but also myself. I carry a piece of each of you within me, and together, you shaped the person I am today. Thank you for not passing me by when you had the opportunity to leave a positive imprint on my life.

To my readers: This book is for you. Thank you for opening your hearts to this exploration of trust, risk, intuition, and fulfillment. My hope is that these pages inspire you to find faith within yourself and take the leap toward a life of deeper meaning and purpose.

And finally, to the divine force that connects us all: Thank you for being the source of endless possibility, grace, and inner strength. This book would not exist without your quiet, unwavering presence. You are perfect in every way.

With deep gratitude,

Terrence

ABOUT THE AUTHOR

Terrence Southern is a robotics, automation, artificial intelligence specialist, entrepreneur, inventor, author, philanthropist and keynote speaker. After earning his Bachelor's degree in Computer Science at Tennessee State University in 2003, his passion for robotics rapidly grew and furthermore propelled him into a nationally recognized leader in the field of Robotics Engineering. As an influencer of innovation and a recognized leader in robotics and artificial intelligence, Mr. Southern continues to implement strategies to deploy robotic solutions and machine learning technology across the globe. Over the course of his 25-year career, he has installed more than 2,000 robots on projects across the world for multiple Fortune 500 companies. Mr. Southern has been the recipient of numerous awards for service to the manufacturing industry and community at large. He is the CEO of Robotopia which delivers cutting-edge industrial automation, robotics and digital manufacturing solutions, alongside comprehensive workforce development training. We revolutionize the way the world's top manufacturers design, produce, and distribute goods, empowering them with smart, scalable technologies and highly skilled talent to drive efficiency, innovation, and growth (www.robo-topia.com). Simultaneously, Terrence is the podcast host of the BlerdOut® Movement where intelligence meets cool and celebrates how the creative minded individuals run the world. Each episode is a celebration of the incredible stories and achievements of global innovators who are shaping the future of technology (www.blerdout. com). He is also the founder of 501c3 Illuminate STEM where the mission is to "illuminate the world" with under-resourced youthful talent in the areas of Science, Technology, Engineering and Math (www.illuminatestem.org). With every accomplishment recognized and every accomplishment achieved silently, Terrence does not rest on his laurels. He is constantly looking for new means by which to stimulate minds and to cultivate our new generation of leaders.

RESOURCES

TERRENCE SOUTHERN

Terrence Southern (www.terrencesouthern.com)

Terrence Southern dedicates his life to the future of technology. His passion for the tech field shines through in all his endeavors. From impactful mentorship, to innovation; Terrence is committed to stimulating minds and cultivating our new generation of leaders. Services provided:

- In-Person & Virtual Keynote Speaking
- Panel Discussions
- Workshop Facilitations
- Podcast Interviews
- Consulting

in @Terrence Southern

@therobobro

@TerrenceSouthern

@therobobro